The Man Who Mistook
His Job
for
a Life

Also by Jonathon Lazear

Meditations for Men Who Do Too Much

Meditations for Parents Who Do Too Much

Remembrance of Father: Words to Heal the Heart

Remembrance of Mother: Words to Heal the Heart

The Man Who Mistook His Job for a Life

A Chronic Overachiever Finds the Way Home

Jonathon Lazear

Crown Publishers

New York

Permissions appear on page 185.

Published by Crown Publishers, New York, New York.
Member of the Crown Publishing Group.

Random House, Inc. New York, Toronto, London, Sydney, Auckland
www.randomhouse.com

CROWN is a trademark and the Crown colophon is a registered trademark of Random House, Inc.

Printed in the United States of America

Design by LENNY HENDERSON

Library of Congress Cataloging-in-Publication Data
Lazear, Jonathon.
The man who mistook his job for a life : a chronic overachiever finds the way home / Jonathon Lazear.—1st ed.
Includes index.
1. Men—Psychology.   2. Masculinity.   3. Workaholism.
4. Workaholics—Rehabilitation.   I. Title.
BF692.5 .L39 2001
155.2'32—dc21   00-065967

ISBN 0-609-60846-0

10   9   8   7   6   5   4   3   2   1

First Edition

For Wendy,
with love always

Cat's in the Cradle

A child arrived just the other day
He came into the world in the usual way
But there were planes to catch and bills to pay
He learned to walk while I was away
And he was talking 'fore I knew it
And as he grew he'd say
I'm gonna be like you, Dad
You know I'm gonna be like you

And the cat's in the cradle and the silver spoon
Little Boy Blue and the Man in the Moon
When you comin' home, Dad?
I don't know when
But we'll get together then, son
You know we'll have a good time then

Well my son turned ten just the other day
He said thanks for the ball, Dad, come on let's play
Can you teach me to throw?
I said not today, I got a lot to do
He said that's okay
And then he walked away but his smile never dimmed
It said I'm gonna be like him
You know I'm gonna be like him

And the cat's in the cradle and the silver spoon
Little Boy Blue and the Man in the Moon
When you comin' home, Dad?
I don't know when
But we'll get together then, son
You know we'll have a good time then

Well he came home from college just the other day
So much like a man I just had to say
Son, I'm proud of you
Can you sit for a while?
He shook his head and he said with a smile
What I'd really like, Dad, is to borrow the car keys
See you later
Can I have them please?

And the cat's in the cradle and the silver spoon
Little Boy Blue and the Man in the Moon
When you coming home, boy?
I don't know when
But we'll get together then, Dad
You know we'll have a good time then

Well I've long since retired, my son's moved away
I called him up just the other day
I said I'd like to see you if you don't mind.
He said I'd love to, Dad, if I could find the time

You see my new job's a hassle and the kids have the flu
But it's sure nice talkin' to you, Dad
It's been sure nice talkin' to you
And as I hung up the phone it occurred to me
He'd grown up just like me
My boy was just like me

And the cat's in the cradle and the silver spoon.
Little Boy Blue and the Man in the Moon
When you coming home, boy?
I don't know when
But we'll get together then, Dad
You know we'll have a good time then

—SANDRA AND HARRY CHAPIN, STORY SONG LTD., ASCAP

Acknowledgments

Thank you . . .

Steve Ross of Crown and my editor, Betsy Rapoport, a brilliant and kind advisor.

Wendy Lazear, who always enhances everything I do.

Ross for typing, editing, and learning.

Mike, who is off on his own adventure.

Christi Cardenas, an invaluable business partner, nearly 'round the clock.

David Rakoff, who came up with the title, when jokingly describing his life to me.

Mary Everson, who saves lives every day.

Al Franken, Evelyn Friedberg, Tim Rumsey, Will Weaver, Leslie Schnur, Tom Spain, Mike Osterholm, Jane Goodall, Jim Sisson, Noah Adams, Scott Simon, Bailey White, Tracy Hickman, Don Perrin, Margaret Weis, Ann Wilson Schaef, R. D. Zimmerman, Pete Hautman, Natalie Goldberg, Tanya Cromey, John Peter Larson, Laura Brinkmeier, Arlene Friedman, Chris and Louise Lazear,

Dennis Cass, Eric Vrooman, Harvey Mackay, Ed Breslin, Terry Gross, Andrei Codrescu, David Brancaccio, Barbara Smith and Dan Gasby, Ray Suarez and others—because friendship is so very important.

Lastly, my apologies to Dr. Oliver W. Sacks, author of many important works, including *The Man Who Mistook His Wife for a Hat*.

Jonathon Lazear

Winter 2001

Minneapolis

Contents

If my heart could do the thinking
and my head began to feel
I would look upon the world anew
and know what's truly real.

— Van Morrison

Out beyond ideas of
wrong-doing and right-doing,
there is a field, I'll
meet you there . . .

— Rumi

Introduction

Why Does Every Man with a Desk Job Carry a Briefcase to and from Home?

We log extra hours at our desk. Our employers expect it, and we expect it of ourselves. But how do we end the workday?

How many of us use the "business dinner" or "cocktail hour" to extend our work and, thus, duck out of going home? As workaholics, we are self-trained avoiders. We know every trick in the book because we wrote it.

Every night I get home in time for dinner, even if on the late side, and my conversation begins with some work-related overview of the day—or more precisely, some diatribe regarding how someone or something didn't go right and how exhausting it all is. This job, these hours, but gee, I'm back at it by 7:30 the next morning.

So often we overextend ourselves on the job because we don't want to face "the second shift." Otherwise we might have to come home, help bathe, feed, and generally take care of the kids. Most of us have abdicated that role; it's easier to hide out at the office.

Times have changed. We know we're supposed to share the responsibilities of the second shift, those hours after work devoted to childrearing. Most of us love our children; that certainly is not the question. But if we get home just in time to read them their bedtime story, then we think we've done our share. Work is the ultimate safe place to hide away from sharing joint custody of the rights of home life.

And let's face it, we're not the type of men who really get a lot out of "nontraditional" feedback. We know when we've outperformed ourselves at the office—it shows in concrete ways, like a vice presidency and a bigger paycheck.

One of the greatest gifts I ever received was when I decided, right on the spot, to walk out of my job back in 1983, even though we had two young sons—one an infant— and barely $2,000 in the bank . . . because it made me look at who I was, and where I'd been, and where I wanted to be.

It was an exciting time. After years of working in the publishing industry in New York, my wife and I took a chance and started our own business in Minneapolis. Even if you have never been an entrepreneur, you know the feeling of embarking on a new job that holds the promise of an exciting career. Every day is exhilarating. Everything seems like a chance to learn something new. We worked tirelessly, around the clock on some days, finding new authors, striking deals, finding more new clients, striking more deals. And it's this exhilaration, to some degree, that acts as a catalyst— the beginning of getting lost in one's work.

As our business grew, we put in fewer hours, but the pressure to produce never left. Even after a string of successful years, there was always the feeling that there was something more we could do, another phone call, another proposal to go over, another client to check in on. You would think that success would bring relief, but instead I started feeling more pressure.

We were living at the top, so to speak. We traveled first class, went to all the places we wanted to; we were "hooked" on success. The bigger the deal, the bigger the client, the bigger the pressure. But when I would start feeling trapped by my job, or angry or resentful of the time it was taking away from my family, I would tell myself that it was only stress, that it was only temporary while a certain deal was getting completed, that it was just part of being a grown-up, a man, an adult who had a family, a job, responsibilities. And just look at those beautiful cars in the garage.

But it wasn't just the "good things," the material stuff, that began the centrifugal force of my burying myself in work and at work. Other, more sinister, things began to accompany this work/life blur. Like hiding out.

Something was wrong with my overachieving life, and it wasn't until I talked to a friend that it started to become clear. He's been my friend for fifteen years. He's a kind, intelligent, introspective, humorous, and dedicated father of three, but he surprised me one night. He told me that as the workday comes to a close and it's nearly time to go home, he begins to feel tense, rigid, worried, vulnerable, helpless, nearly in a panic.

This is a man who loves his wife and kids, and who practices his religion weekly. He's known in the community for his humanity and selflessness. He's been interviewed and portrayed on television largely for those same values. He even makes a "good living," so his wife doesn't need to work, nor does he have to scrape to send his young adult children to private school. Every night, though, he's tense, and the mere thought of anticipating home—the kids, their (appropriate) demands, his spouse and her needs—nearly sends him into an anxiety attack. He feels he isn't "safe" when he gets home. "It's not work," he said. "It's not where I can be comfortable; it's not what I know."

He loves his family as much or more than any husband and father I've ever known. And at first I tried to comfort him, feeling that his problems were his and not mine, that I might be able to offer some consolation. But the longer we talked, the more I realized that his problems *were* mine. I realized that I also sought shelter in work, not because I didn't love my family, but because work offered a place where I felt the most confident, the most competent. Even the most needed.

We talked about how we knew how to act at work, but who were we at home? Work was so much easier, so much clearer, the rules simpler somehow. But home—or life with friends, or family, or community—that was all governed by strange rules, filled with complications and uncertainties. We talked and talked about the pressures of family life, and how lost we felt, a conversation that, if it had been about work, would have been perfectly ordinary for two men to have, but because it wasn't about work, it felt new. And then the strangest thing happened. We both realized that a lot of times when we were stressed, it wasn't because of work. Work was nothing. What was really stressful was everything *but* work. Our jobs, as demanding as they were, were actually the safest place to hide from the realities of life. That exciting career had actually become a trap.

My friend mentioned that scientists have identified a phenomenon called the Stockholm syndrome, in which very often a victim of a kidnapping or a prisoner who has been incarcerated begins to "cross over" and show respect, sometimes even love, for the kidnapper or the guard. It's kind of like that when work becomes a place to find refuge, he told me.

After talking to my friend, the work-related problems in my own life became more clear. I started thinking about the role of work in my life and saw how easy it was to have fallen into a trap. If you've picked up this book, you're probably struggling with the same questions and doubts. Your job has become such a big part of your life that it dwarfs everything else. There is no denying the satisfaction it can bring, but you're also wondering if it isn't taking from you more than it's giving. You've spun a web that defines but also conceals you. It is your salvation and your damnation—you're living inside the job and whether it makes you unhappy or fulfilled almost doesn't matter anymore, because you feel it's your only choice.

And when you look at your life, you see the moments, the symptoms of being a man who mistakes his job for a life. Like I did, you feel exhausted even after a full night's sleep. Or you can't sleep at night, because you lie awake replaying a phone conversation you had earlier that day or mentally rehearsing one you're going to have tomorrow. Or maybe whenever you meet a new group of people, you focus only on what those people do; the only thing you can talk about at parties is your job or someone else's. Or maybe you get angry at your spouse when you're really angry at your boss. Or maybe you simply come home and don't have the energy for anything else.

As a man who mistook his job for a life, I have coped by remaining aloof, even silent. I have been an emotional isolationist, fleeing the real and imagined ever-present jury— my coworkers, my peers, my family, my wife, even my children. Sometimes I felt combative and aggressive, but mostly I was lost, unfeeling, unresponsive. And like you, I felt like I didn't have a choice. Downsizing, rightsizing, and just plain career terror had me clinging to my job for dear life. "Choice" is not in the vocabulary of the man who mistakes his job for a life. "The good father and husband" is the "good provider." How often have we heard that? Or if we're not providing, if we're not lost in duty, we're lost in ambition. We are highly competitive, hypervigilant. We see a parade of MBAs and fast-talkers dance through the office, and we know we can prove that we're even better than they are! But where are our values? What happened to the dreams that used to keep us going?

Once I had identified what was wrong, my immediate thought was, *How had this happened?* Was there a moment, a deciding action or reaction that created all this confusion between work and self? I recalled a particularly stressful time when I had recently signed a celebrity client. I was certain that my problems with work had started then. But then I thought back to a previous time, and then farther back and then farther back. Finally I arrived at the moment I had started the agency and decided that was the moment I crossed over.

In fact, there is no one "moment of crossing over." There are actions, reactions, and inferences that reinforce men's loss of self over a period of time. A long period of time. The more I started reading about workaholism and about the problems in the workplace that face men in particular, the more I realized that this wasn't a problem that started with that first big promotion. My plight had a long history. The breakthrough conversation I had with my friend wasn't catalyzed by a bad day at the office, or even by a bad year. It had been building for a long time.

It had started with something as simple as being asked,

constantly, sometimes jokingly, sometimes seriously, what I wanted to be when I grew up. Adults start prepping young boys for their first job interview long before they have even gone off to preschool. These are minor life moments, but they are pervasive and insistent, and it prepares a young man well for a life in which his job defines his identity.

We all heard those seemingly harmless stock questions when the grown-ups approached us at the latest party or family gathering. "What do you want to be when you grow up? Maybe a fireman? An astronaut? A policeman?" They were the standard way in which uncomfortable adults entered into conversations with equally uncomfortable children. In my case, the questions centered on my very early interest in drawing; I drew houses, buildings, cut-aways of apartment buildings, and later (by the age of three) cars, cars, cars. Which led virtually everyone to expect that if I didn't work for General Motors, then I'd teach art, or be a great architect. Barely out of kinder-garten, and everyone seemed to know what I was going to be. And the die was cast. In the blink of an eye, it seems, I was off to college to earn my bachelor of arts. I wanted very much to live up to the expectations my parents and those close to me had.

On the way to becoming an architect, I hit a speed bump called math. No aptitude. No interest. Uh-oh. What was I if I wasn't the architect everyone wanted me to be? I was already defining myself by what I did—or at least what everyone said I should do—instead of who I was, and I was barely out of my teens.

Like Father, Like Son

My father wasn't a good example of separating his identity from his job or his work from his home. He housed his office—you guessed it—at home. In an age when more and more workers are "going solo" and working from a new home office, allow me to warn you: If you don't create clear-cut borders between your home life and your home office, your office will win every time. My father would often return after dinner to his office, a few short steps away from the dining room to continue working, often late into the night. Since he had chosen to put work before family, he was often irritated by being interrupted during the evening hours for family matters.

We were a little mixed up on the work/home boundary issue, to put it mildly. One message, however, that came through loud and clear to me was that my father was working any and all hours to put us through private school and provide, provide, provide.

I knew my father was in the house, but I felt his presence only indirectly. My mother would call to him, "Jon, are you coming up?" (Yes, I'm Jon, Junior—another source of the pressure of expectations.) His offices were then in the basement of our house. "Jon," my mother would call to him again, "When are you going to come up here?" I knew she felt abandoned. That's probably why I began to feel him more as a ghostly presence than as a flesh-and-blood father. Looking back, why didn't I make a mental note not to disappear the way he had?

The Courage to Change

Once I realized that my problems with work were so deep-seated, it was almost a relief. It meant it was serious, and that it would take some time to fix, but it was also reassuring, knowing that lots of men out there, like me, had been dealing with the pressure of work since before they were even working. The changing roles of men—professionally, politically, and personally—are massive. In the past forty years, men and their relationships with everything from their cars to their choice of underwear have been the fodder for psychoanalysts and talk-show hosts. It's enough to render us helpless, angry, and afraid, but this is also a hopeful time, because the issues men and men alone face are being taken seriously. There are hundreds of ways men can reestablish a sense of themselves and their own humanity, and we can do it without going to sweat lodges, beating our chests, and howling at the moon.

It takes effort (notice I'm trying not to use the word *work*), but it can be done. I'm not going to sugarcoat it. Change is difficult, maybe the most difficult thing. I wanted to write this book and share my story to help show you how, so you can not only learn more about the way men get lost in their work, but what you can do about it. Men, as we know, are taught to think, not feel. We don't have time to feel. We can pretend at birthday parties, weddings, funerals, and family reunions, but there's a not-so-subtle backbeat that plays underneath the smile and embarrassed laughter we share in order to appear engaged. What we need is practice, and not just with feeling, but with taking the time to recognize where we are, and what we're doing with our lives. It's not easy in this 24 hour, 7 days a week, 365 days a year life, where we are never far from a fax machine or a computer terminal, where there is always another e-mail to be sent out or a ringing phone to pick up, but we can learn to reclaim long-dormant behaviors and feelings—doing the things that make us feel "real"—and become men who truly enjoy our families and friends, men who have a healthy attitude toward work.

A few years ago, I took my first real vacation in years. No phone number where clients could reach me in an emergency, no book proposals brought along, no magazines to scour for writers who might make good clients. Nothing but my wife and children, the reasons why I had quit that job in the first place, back in 1983, when everything was filled with hope. It had been a long journey to get to that point, where I could actually enjoy something as simple as a vacation, when I could completely resist the temptation to turn a sunny beach into just another office environment.

You, too, can find the way home.

Chapter 1

The Best Little Boy in the World

Dad Works So Hard

I remember that my father was absent more than he was home. And when he was home, he revealed little about who he was, although we heard in conversations between my mother and him quite a bit about what he did.

When I think about the time when I was six or seven years old growing up in Ohio, my strongest memories of my father are of him leaving for work either to his office in downtown Columbus or to his home office. It wasn't just that he was home less than he was at work. There was something important about the ritual of him preparing for work on any given day. He was off to do important things. He was off to do business, to work, to provide for us. Our mother made it clear to my sister, my brother, and to me that HE WAS WORKING. It wasn't really important what he "did," but that he was working, and work was something you talked about very seriously.

This is a common pattern. If Dad works long hours, we excuse his retreat from the family. He missed dinner again: "He's working so hard, he couldn't get home in time." He ducked out on vacations: "Dad will be here on the weekend; he had to stay home and work. After all, he paid for this vacation." He was a no-show at school meetings: "Dad has to be out of town those days; no one else at work can fill his shoes." He ducked in and out of the family get-togethers: "Dad's on the phone again—they just can't seem to run their company without him." Countless meals were interrupted in our home by business calls; work came first—there were no boundaries between the "home office" and home. When it came to work, our family was always ready to make excuses for Dad not being there. And that excuse was always work.

My father was self-employed. That meant he didn't have bosses in the traditional sense of the word. However, he was a sales representative, which meant, among other things, that he actually had a number of bosses because he represented five or six manufacturing companies. He had to make those men happy with his performance, and had to make his customers happy, too. Making all those people happy took a great deal of work. He was always overseeing some near-catastrophe, real or imagined, lest these folks be unhappy for a single moment.

If his leaving in the morning was an important ritual, waiting for Dad to come home had an air of expectation. Did he have a good day? Or a bad one? Was there some crisis left at the office that would cast a shadow over the night? Because even if Dad wasn't outright angry about work, even if he didn't take it out on his family as mine sometimes did, if Dad had a bad or unproductive day, we had to be respectful of it. No one would have dared to challenge him on this: "Come on, Dad, maybe it wasn't so bad," or "Gee, Dad, maybe you can just solve the problem the way you solved all the others." Work was something magical and difficult and not to be shrugged off. It was mystery and tyranny all wrapped together in his life.

The sad part was that in making all those people happy, my father was rarely around for us—to be made happy or not. We never wanted for anything, at least not materially. What I found out as I was growing up is that all we wanted was him. But what we got was his anger and his frustration about his work, which swallowed up most of any time he might have had for us. It wasn't an act of cruelty or dishonesty. He simply did not know how to interact with his children, or often our mother, or even in superficial social situations with friends (and he didn't have any to speak of). The center of his attention was his business, as it was his father's and, most probably, his grandfather's.

One of his ways of decompressing after a day's work was to watch Walter Cronkite's *CBS News*, which he would verbally annotate for the entire half hour. He talked backed to the television because he often felt so ineffectual at work. Much of his anger and frustration played out in his running dialogue with newscasters. I've talked to a lot of men with similar memories. The success of the balance of the day rested on the answer to the $64,000 question: Had Dad had a good day or a bad day? If Dad had had a bad day, we intuitively backed off, Mom swept in with a drink and sympathy, and we kept our distance until the coast was clear. If Dad had had a good day, we could fly into his arms, share some happy news, or maybe dump our own problems—the brother who'd been mean to us, the best friend who wouldn't play with us, the bad test score, how we'd blown it on the soccer or football field. We should have been longing to see our Dad turn up the sidewalk or pull into the driveway, but a lot of us waited with a sense of trepidation, even fear. Sometimes we were relieved when he had to work late again—relieved at not having to walk around on tiptoe and whisper to give Dad a break after his hard day. It was just easier not to be on guard.

My father knew no "normal" office hours. Nor did we. You could find him at his desk at 9:30 at night and at 7:00 the next morning. I knew that he worked incredibly hard. He sacrificed himself for us. He was largely anonymous, but loved for what he provided for us. He was desperately unhappy, but we didn't really recognize it because there was virtue in his immersion in his work. To make matters even more convoluted, my mother began to work for him as his "right hand" (read: secretary). So now we got the same message twice: "We're both killing ourselves here, but look at the schools you're attending and the cars in the garage."

We all have an image of Americans in the fifties glorying in cocktail parties and backyard barbecues and taking long, lazy motor trips across the country. Europe opened up as a tourist destination, and Disneyland beckoned us. But my parents socialized little, or when they did, it was often work related. My family took few vacations.

The Virtuous Worker

The hypocrisy of working all the time to be able to enjoy life may be obvious to some, but not to all of us. In our house, we were made aware, intentionally or not, of how privileged and truly fortunate we were to have the home we had, the clothes we wore, the way we were perceived by the community. We felt every effort and the energy my father expended to provide for us. I honestly don't believe my parents were aware of how intensely they transmitted this value to us.

I remember my own birthday parties as a child. They were always well planned and a great time for the guests. My father would be present for perhaps the first hour, but would then slip away to his office because he had an important call to return or an order to finalize. His hard work allowed me, year after to year, to receive incredible gifts—the best bike, a television for my room (extravagant then), even a car when I turned sixteen. It sounds cliché, but as welcome as the gifts were, I would have been much happier to have had him there as an active participant in the gathering.

Looking back now, I realize how uncomfortable he would have been in this social situation. He, too, was a man who mistook his job for a life. This is why my parents would so often discuss work at dinner, during a drive to see my grandparents, or even on Christmas eve—there were no "sacred moments" reserved for family. The house was a beehive; a place of business—the work ethic observed night and day. The backdrop of my life involved carbon paper, files, phone calls, typewriters humming, and the house smelling of Pine-Sol and Spic and Span. But for all the buzz, there was often little else. Take away the work, take away the activity, and what did we have? If you're not careful, that's what hard work and dedication can get you: a house full of unhappy people, waiting for the mailman. We unconsciously absorbed a crucial equation:

Virtue = Work

So, you do the math. Dad's life really is about work. Dad is his job. Dad is not Dad unless he's away, or on the phone, or at the office. And Dad is to be admired; why, he's a positive saint, he works so hard. If I ever thought my father's obsession with work would teach me otherwise, it didn't. I admired my father's ethic and, like any child, desperately wanted his approval. Like it or not, I became a facsimile of my father. My father was not solely to blame for this, nor was my mother. It goes beyond the home.

What Do You Want to Be?

Earlier I mentioned the ritual of asking children what they want to be when they grow up. Of course, little girls and little boys both get the question. However, no one ever asks a boy: How many children do you want to have? Or: What kind of a home would you like to live in? Or: What do you think will make you happy?

Sadly, most of these questions are thought to be "feminine" questions. The questions asked of boys focus on what they want to be, not who, or how, or why. So from an early age, we begin to dehumanize our sons, prizing them for attaining non-family-centered achievements; winning trophies, races, games; and yes, ultimately, working and providing for themselves and others.

It took me years to figure out how unhappy my parents were, slaving away under their self-imposed requirements for what needed to be done. At the time, I didn't know any better, and I even liked the business. It made me feel important, too. And so when my dad would ask me what I wanted to be when I grew up, even if I didn't know, I would always have an answer. That answer would always be something that I thought would make him proud.

Little boys (and little girls) learn a great deal by observation, aping and mimicking the behaviors of their parents and adults they admire. And what we learn is that being busy indicates work, which is virtuous. I wanted to be loved, to be seen as virtuous, so I copied some of my dad's behaviors. I got busy, or at least learned how to appear busy. I really wasn't "producing" anything. My schoolwork showed that I wasn't too busy. I was busy being away from the house. I wanted to be away all day, and all night. I didn't want to be in a place where joy was suspect—where watching TV was seen as a total waste of time, where if you didn't have a "project," you were told you were "at loose ends." Even at that early age, I learned to inflate how busy I was. If I had a book report due, it didn't matter how hard it was to do, what was important was to make it seem hard and time consuming and in need of my full attention. I've had friends whose fathers regarded their reading books as wasting time, and one whose father sent him out to the yard to pick up sticks if he caught his son watching Saturday morning cartoons. ("Don't you have anything better to do?") I had another friend whose dad was always up by 6:30 every day on the weekend to get an early jump on the house chores. The message we all internalized was a more modern version of "Idle hands are the Devil's workshop." Ah, the great escape into the garage . . .

But even for all my best acting efforts, my father and mother knew that schoolwork wasn't all that hard, and they made sure we knew it too. They were always very clear, and not in a harsh way, but in a very restrained way, that the work adults did was much harder, more demanding, with so much more at stake: "Just wait until you have children of your own." It was demeaning. I couldn't live up to my father's idea of productivity. None of us could.

Gradually, like a lot of kids, I learned how to coast. But I knew if I continued, I'd not only lose any respect my father had for me, I'd also not be "successful." And so I realized, probably when I was just about to hit puberty, that I wanted to be the best little boy in the world. And I set out to prove I would be. Because I was already the "peacekeeper" in the family, it only made sense that I'd also be the most "productive," and gain further favor. I just had to figure out what kind of work I'd do, how much of it would make me virtuous, and think about how my father would respect me for working myself to death. I was the self-appointed "good child" in the family—and I proved it by being very successful. I had no idea what it would cost.

Self-Disciplined, Self-Directed, Self-Centered Young Man Seeks Same

When I got my first job, I discovered firsthand that work can set you free. You make your own money, and you don't depend on any other source—and that's liberating. Our first job is a major signpost of adulthood.

Along with my paycheck, I got a whole new set of "supervisors" to appease and please. During high school, I worked in one of those huge toy stores, in the stockroom. I hated it, but I felt I couldn't quit. It would let my parents down. That's how crazy it is. I was making $1.75 an hour, walking up three-story ladders to retrieve Barbie and Ken dolls. Risking my life for Mattel and my parents.

But I was rewarded. My father was proud of his son who had both an after-school and a weekend job.

Once I started working, I never stopped. Between then and graduation, I worked after school and then had a summer minicareer. The jobs were demanding. I wanted it that way. The more demanding, the better.

I worked through high school. I worked through college. When I got to graduate school, which I never finished, I worked in a bookstore. This led to my first "big" job managing an entire store for a larger chain. Bingo! That's when I could work twelve to fifteen hours a day. My exhaustion was exhilarating. I was hooked.

During college, it had become clearer that grades mattered less than the question of what to do with my life. If I was going to make my father proud, I'd have to pick something to do. I wanted to study art, but being an artist isn't a "real" profession, or so I was led to believe (not just by him). I had my ideals, but they were the shaky ideals of a young man, not the seasoned beliefs of someone older who has fought for how he wants to live. The closer I got to college graduation, the more I realized that despite all these piddling jobs, I didn't really know anything about being in the workplace. I was playing at it, not really doing it. For all the time spent watching my mother and father worry about work, I still had no idea what work was, what it meant to work. Work for me was just about keeping my head down and getting it done. Fulfillment never occurred to me.

Once I got my managing job, I started learning two lessons. First, that a lot of what I thought was important about work, wasn't. Every job involved a lot of busywork and work that went nowhere, but by working hard, a lot of people were able to survive and support families. Second, and more important, I learned that when work did lead to something bigger (a good investment, a new product that was successful, a best-selling author), there were incredible rewards. There seemed to be two choices. You could work hard just to survive, or work hard and strive and try to reap the rewards. Either way, the message was that you had to work hard.

Birth of a Yuppie Puppy

After my stint with working all hours for a largely uninterested company and boss (after all, what self-respecting workaholic doesn't want some notice?), I got a job in publishing.

Now, most people are not interested in the day-to-day inner workings of book publishing, but let me just say that for a budding workaholic, it was Valhalla. I learned, while at the beginning of what was termed "Yuppiedom," that I'd need to throw myself into my work if I wanted a prayer of succeeding. In publishing, in order to rise to the top, you had to routinely sacrifice evenings, weekends, even vacations. You were expected to use most of your "spare time" reading and evaluating manuscripts; keeping up with the entertainment trade magazines and newspapers; editing endless piles of manuscripts; and being available for authors to vent to on the phone twenty-four hours a day. I don't know how many weekends I spent telephonically "hot-walking" the famous, the infamous, and the self-important. But I don't delude myself: it was my choice. I didn't want to be the one to miss the next bestseller by leaving it on the submissions shelf at my office for an extra day or two. What if someone else preempted it under my nose? I didn't want to be the one to anger the big-time author by not chatting him up at 11:30 at night. What if the editorial director assigned him to another publicist? I wanted to be a player in the hot book auctions, to lunch with the top literary agents, to see my name in the "News" section of *Publishers Weekly*, the trade rag that all my fellow strivers read.

So I gladly put in the hours; I'd long ago learned how to do that. And I began to be amply rewarded. At a relatively young age, I began moving rather rapidly up the ladder. I got noticed. I got job offers. I worked until all hours, and basked in what I thought was the limelight. I was one of the young Turks making things happen. But the funny thing was, by the time I was in my late twenties, I began to feel burned out. And then the unthinkable happened. I got fired (!) from a very prestigious job at a prestigious publishing house. I got fired because I didn't know what I was doing. I hadn't been given any direction by my superior, no help, no guidance. But in all candor, I hadn't exactly been begging for help either; I had my pride, and I figured if I just kept my nose to the grindstone, I could make it work out. I thought if I put in enough hours, my boss would notice and assume I was dedicated and busy. In truth, I was floundering, in over my head, and scared to death.

My boss was less than sensitive, and I believed that in some sick way, he wanted me to fail. It was, in general, a ruthless, cutthroat place to work. We used to say that "they" didn't wait for you to turn around, "they" stabbed you in the *front.*

A workplace like this is perfect for bringing up young workaholics. I failed upward, hands down.

I could have taken the firing as an opportunity to stop and think about what I was doing. Was I happy in the job?

Did I want to pursue some other career? Had I learned anything from my mistakes? Did I have any short-term or long-term goals? After all, I'd rushed from job to job from my teen years on, and it would have made a lot of sense to devote some time to introspection and self-examination. But I didn't give it a moment's thought. I entertained some fleeting thoughts of panic and humiliation, but then leaped right back into the job hunt on the publishing track. After a brief (one-week) hiatus, I landed another job. No one focused on my failure; they focused on my successes, so I was motivated to plow right ahead and make more of them. And now I could do it with an even loftier title, and more money. More money—now there's another great trap.

But I did learn one thing from being fired. Whether we work hard to survive or work hard to succeed, we learn quickly that we're more richly rewarded for being "doers" rather than "thinkers." A man who makes decisions quickly and unwaveringly is perceived as more masculine. He who hesitates looks unsure of himself, his intellect, his power, or his place. He's not being careful or considerate; he's a follower instead of a leader. Making a snap judgment on a situation or a person is our stock in trade. After all, we have so much to do, we don't have the time, and certainly not the inclination, to ponder, to weigh, to assess.

Most of us saw our fathers make quick decisions. "Yes!" or "No!" No discussion, just laying down the law. Were they ever afraid? Did they ever have doubts? Of course. Everyone's afraid when they make a decision, no matter how calm their exterior may be. But you can never show yourself to be equivocating. Because you work all the time, because you're dedicated to making important decisions throughout any given day, you can't hesitate. You aren't allowed to. Plus there is power in that seeming self-assuredness. The real motivation may be cowardice, impatience, boredom, or fear that makes us come to such instantaneous conclusions, but no one ever questions the posture of knowingness. I quickly learned that it was better to be quick with the wrong answer than to appear slow with the right one.

Pride is another smokescreen we have to nurture as we move out of those early jobs and really start taking hold of success. If I know everything, why would I need to ponder anything or ask anyone for help? Excessive pride doesn't mean you get lost in your work, but it does seal the trap once you fall in. Because you're too proud to think, or too proud to ask for help, you turn to what you do and, ironically, the pride in what you do to define yourself. The product of your work, what you turn out—whether it's a perfectly ironed garment, a car tuned and aligned for the Indy 500, or the finely sharpened scalpel ready for the most delicate surgery—becomes what defines you.

I met my wife through the publishing business—surprise. Wendy had, at a young age, attained a prestigious job at a major movie studio, was highly paid, and moved among movie stars and other powerful figures. Her persona drew me to her. How could I resist? Here was an upwardly mobile, very attractive movie executive who appeared to be totally self-confident and a fellow worker bee—the perfect partner.

We married, both on virtually the same rung of the ladder upward. For a long time, we were equal hard-chargers. Our work was highly social. Most evenings found us either in our offices or wining or dining clients.

Our first son, Michael, was born in 1979. Wendy made the decision to stay at home and take care of him. We moved to the deep suburbs of New Jersey while I continued to commute into Manhattan. The commute was hellishly long; I rarely saw anything of my newborn son in the daytime. I'd leave in the morning, in the dark, and he'd usually be asleep. I'd get home in the dark, and he'd be asleep again.

In 1982, Ross came along, and we had moved from the hot zone of Manhattan to Minneapolis. There, Wendy and I started our own literary agency. We'd be our own bosses, create our own lives, rather than having them dictated by others. We'd do it "our way."

"Our way" turned out to be "my way." I was up at bat all day and into the night. Wendy was on hand, and certainly helped launch what became a very solid business, but when she disappeared for the second shift with the kids, it was once again time for me to grab the reins and disappear into work, and who would stop me? Certainly not me.

I became addicted to doing big deals. If I felt trapped or isolated, I could always do another deal and point to it as proof that I didn't need anybody. I relied on my own taste, my own judgment, and my own sense of creativity. I not only had to work long hours, I wanted to. I allowed myself to get completely lost in my work. And who would question that? I was gaining notoriety; I'd gone from being a small fish in the big pond of New York publishing to a big fish in the small pond of literary agents in Minneapolis. My successes— the hefty five- and six-figure deals for my author clients, and all the publicity write-ups that followed—fueled my ongoing love affair with my desk and phone. And then more and more money began to appear. Wow! This nonstop work was really paying off, but at what cost?

Burned Out

More money. More status. More emotional distance. More self-justification. More hiding out from the family. I was isolating myself just like alcoholics do. I was turning into one cold fish, rarely showing warmth or interest in my wife or family, but I was still the stellar provider.

Add everything up—the long hours, the constant avail-ability, the pride in work—and you aren't necessarily a workaholic, just like you can't count the number of drinks you have at a party and decide you have a drinking problem. If you're working at full tilt, with no downtime to regroup and replenish your energy levels, you realize deep down that you're in danger. You're "running on empty," as the Jackson Browne song says. But you don't stop to gauge how serious the problem is. It's easy to ignore a problem if you don't know how to quantify it. At some point, I stumbled across the kind of reality check that forced me to take stock; it's called the Pines and Aronson Burnout Scale. Answer the following questions, then add up your score to see if you're in danger of burning out.

How often do you have any of the following experiences?

Please use the scale:

1 = Never	5 = Often
2 = Once in a great while	6 = Usually
3 = Rarely	7 = Always
4 = Sometimes	

_____ 1. Being tired

_____ 2. Feeling depressed

_____ 3. Having a good day

_____ 4. Being physically exhausted

_____ 5. Being emotionally exhausted

_____ 6. Being happy

_____ 7. Being wiped out

_____ 8. Feeling like you can't take it anymore

_____ 9. Being unhappy

_____ 10. Feeling run down

____ 11. Feeling trapped

____ 12. Feeling worthless

____ 13. Being weary

____ 14. Being troubled

____ 15. Feeling disillusioned and resentful

____ 16. Being weak and susceptible to illness

____ 17. Feeling hopeless

____ 18. Feeling rejected

____ 19. Feeling optimistic

____ 20. Feeling energetic

____ 21. Feeling anxious

To compute your score, add the values you wrote next to numbers 1, 2, 4, 5, 8, 9, 10, 11, 12, 13, 14, 15, 16, 17, 18, 21. Total = ____ (A).

Add the values you wrote next to numbers 3, 6, 9, 19, 20. Total = ____ (B).

Subtract (B) from 32. Total = ____ (C).

Add A and C. Total = ____ (D).

Divide D by 21. Total = ____. This is your burnout score.

Interpreting your score:

If you scored from 2 to 3, you're doing well.

If you scored between 3 and 4, you may be at risk for burnout.

If your score is higher than 4, you're experiencing burnout.

Adapted from Ayala Pines and Elliot Aronson, *Career Burnout: Causes & Cures* (New York: Free Press, 1981).

As with alcoholism, there are warning signs of workaholism, although they are not so obvious. My problem was that my business was becoming more successful, which seemed to justify the hours and the time away from my family. But then even when I wasn't busy (for example, during December, when New York publishing is notoriously quiet), I still behaved like I was striving, climbing, pushing to succeed, and because it was all in service of work, no one could say anything. If I had ten drinks at a party, my wife would pull me aside and talk to me about it. But work an extra ten hours over the weekend, and who will stop you? Men who victimize themselves in this way are almost always praised as overachievers. The certain truth is that although they appear to be productive, many are grossly unhappy, under-appreciated, and have low self-esteem. Because that is ultimately the truth we all find. That it's not how much you work, but how working so much makes you feel that counts. And how I felt was miserable.

Work and Narcissism

Sometimes workaholism is considered self-reliance, but what it really turns out to be, more often than not, is narcissism. Not all men who lose themselves in their work are narcissists. But men who are very occupied with themselves—mostly through their accomplishments—are like the Greek figure

Narcissus, always looking into the water and falling in love with his own reflection. That's a lonely occupation, but for many, it's the only way they know how to live.

I was becoming addicted to my public persona. The one that made it appear that I was *the* publishing guru between the west and east coasts. A Player with a capital *P*. The one that answered me back from my photograph in newspapers, local and national magazines, even television shows. I was rubbing elbows with all the "right people" in town and on both coasts. That was my brand of narcissism, brought on largely by workaholism.

The hardest part of work narcissism is recognizing it in yourself. Again, because it's work, because the product of your problem isn't a hangover but a paycheck, it's hard to recognize when you're doing something as much to satisfy your own vanity as to provide for others. I thought I was doing something good for my family, but when I took a hard look at myself, I realized I was mainly doing it for myself.

When men become overly invested in themselves, it doesn't leave much room for anything, or anyone. It wasn't that I wasn't in the world at large. Indeed, I probably believed that the world and everything and everyone in it was there for me. I set my standards by my vanities. My sense of self-worth became, in short, my world.

When you get caught up in what you think your image is, as opposed to what it really is, you blur the lines between physical narcissism, mental narcissism, and "player" narcissism. I should have remembered what they tell people in the news: "Don't believe what they say about you in the newspapers." When you become your work or your career, you pretty much automatically become shallow. Why? Because there's no room in your world for anyone except you. That was exactly what was happening to me.

Now that Wendy was so involved with the kids, I could begin to drive into work earlier and earlier, and only come up for air late at night, sometimes after everyone else was long asleep. Now that I could immerse myself more fully in my business, miraculously the opportunities to do so multiplied. Suddenly, it seemed I almost always had to fly to New York on business, to L.A. for other business, occasionally drive to meet prospective clients, and take other two-day trips here or there. After all, it was all part of ramping up to make us rich, carefree, and happy.

After a few days at a five-star hotel in Beverly Hills meeting with interesting, talented people (it was easy to call this work), I would come home and voilà—there was more work to do waiting for me back at my office. I'd drive back in and disappear, citing the fact that "no one can do what I do, and I was gone for a few days, and now all this work has piled up."

In various studies on workaholism, it has been shown that men who are lost in their work for fifty or more hours a week are not particularly "smart workers." So, it's not just productivity that suffers but, of course, the man who is so immersed in his work that he has mistaken his life for his job. Fifty hours was a light work week for me. Sixty was more like it.

Stretched to the limit. That's how I felt. As the business grew and I became more reclusive, I couldn't be faulted (or so I thought) because even though I was emotionally distant, I was bringing in a seven-figure income.

For a long time, I didn't see that I was losing out, because I couldn't see what work was doing to me. Because there were no limits on how much I could work, no cleaning crews turning out the lights when it was time to close up shop, I worked and worked and worked. But it's not just a numbers game. A workaholic could work fifty hours a week, while a perfectly healthy (but very busy) person could work sixty hours. The difference is that the person working sixty could still remain connected to his family, his children, his community; he could put them first, and work second. The man who mistakes his job for a life clings to work. It happened so insidiously that I almost didn't recognize it until it was too late.

Chapter 2

Check Yourself: Are You a Workaholic?

The chickens have come home to roost . . .

Recently, the NASDAQ has, essentially, fallen through the ice. Many of the dot.coms that flourished in the past decade are either in serious trouble or have disappeared.

So, what do we do now? Some of us were practically minting money online.

Do we become hysterical, take two jobs (if we can find two jobs), and try to cover our debts and our egos?

The economy is always in a state of flux. We get lulled into a sense of false security during the good times. But now (and in the future), we hit the wall. It is a perfect time for workaholics to go into overdrive. A perfect time for the ambitious to lose themselves in the search for work that will equal what was lost . . . both the mythology and the reality.

We think and dream in black and white. We deal in absolutes. Positive or negative. There's no in-between for us. Guilty or innocent.

The world, however, is in vivid color, and people, work, and yes, even the market, are subject to change. We need to think about the "grays" in our lives and how few things are black or white.

Obsession with our work, careers, and jobs has never been so pervasive as it is today.

Nearly everything we see outside of our work is enabling us to overachieve—to work harder and harder, make more and more—as a recent *Newsweek* magazine cover story put it, "I'm So Angry—Everyone's Rich But Me!"

And then there's the blur between home and workplace. So many of us take calls that are not appropriate, blurring the lines between our work and our downtime. Our lack of boundaries creates the need to be "de-depressed" with medication, while we leave the myths of "the good provider" as legacies to our children.

Make no mistake—workaholism is an addiction. If those of us afflicted with it don't do something to curb our insatiable thirst to immerse ourselves in our jobs, the jobs will kill us, and we will have pulled the trigger. Work addiction robs us of ourselves—and those who love us. Just as gin and cocaine can tear a marriage apart, ruin all family relationships, and isolate the user, so can this malady that is at once deplored and celebrated.

When I was deep in my own problems with workaholism, I would have groaned at the idea of taking the following quiz. Who has the time? Aren't there more important things to do? And if I'm sick, why I can't I just take the cure? Give me the pill, quick, or the "Top Ten Things to Do to Cure My Workaholism." That's part of what is so pernicious about any addiction, whether it's to alcohol, drugs, sex, or work— the addiction keeps you from knowing how bad you've gotten, from knowing how sick you are. Addictions are illnesses masquerading as coping mechanisms.

What makes work addiction even harder to diagnose is that it's normally a very legitimate way to spend your day. Think of all the people around you at work. Picture that person down the hall busy typing away, trying to meet a deadline; how would you know if he is suffering from workaholism? How would you make the diagnosis? And even more importantly, how does he know if he doesn't take the time to find out?

The following quiz is a tool, nothing more, but if you allow yourself to use it, it can be invaluable. There are benefits to simply taking the quiz, to reading each question, and answering honestly. Don't let yourself race through it quickly (because as I've said, we're prized for our speedy decision making) so you can rush to add up your score. The final tally will give insight into your attitudes toward work, but not as much as taking the time with each question.

It's not the final answer that matters, but the way you arrive at it. Workaholism wears many masks, and the way it hides who you really are is different from how it hid who I was. The following questions try to get at the root of a number of symptoms of workaholism, such as anger, problems with sleep, and emotional detachment. Think of them less as traditional test questions, where there is a right and wrong answer, and more like rhetorical questions, like a big game of Would You Rather?—that party stalwart where you try to decide between two undesirable choices. All the questions taken together will help you see patterns in your life, but sometimes all it takes is one question and your entire life is revealed.

A Self-Test for Workaholics

If you think you may be overboard at work, and your daily stress level is off the map, please use this scale to take the quiz:

5 = yes, absolutely
4 = yes, most of the time
3 = occasionally
2 = rarely, if ever
1 = never

1. a) I have a short temper and am quick to rile.

     1   2   3   4   5

b) I am often just below the boiling point—and could blow any minute.

1   2   3   4   5

c) I feel that anger is part of my psychological makeup—part of me—and I can't break free.

1   2   3   4   5

d) I keep myself burdened by grudges that ultimately take the form of anger.

1   2   3   4   5

e) Anger is almost always a motivating force in my decision making.

1   2   3   4   5

f) I have a very short fuse when I encounter mistakes and oversights that others foist on me.

1   2   3   4   5

g) My anger often inhibits my focus on any given task; it enables my scattered thinking.

1   2   3   4   5

h) When there are important errors made at work, I'm always certain they've been made by others.

1   2   3   4   5

TOTAL _____

2. a) My sleep patterns are erratic, and I have trouble getting to sleep and waking refreshed.

1   2   3   4   5

b) I have a sense of dread that overcomes me like a shroud when I think about my financial obligations, and whether or not I'll be able to meet them.

1   2   3   4   5

c) I'm generally uncomfortable around my peers in social situations; I feel anxious and inadequate.

1   2   3   4   5

d) I feel unsettled when changes are made at work or at home; I need the status quo to keep me from an emotional lapse.

1   2   3   4   5

e) I'm at an age now where I feel angry, anxious, and threatened by any new employer or coworker who is younger than me, especially if his performance is seen to be remarkable.

1   2   3   4   5

f) I've grown away from the alliances and friendships I have had at work and do not look for new ones.

1   2   3   4   5

TOTAL _____

3. a) I don't feel "listened to," or valued at home, by my spouse or my kids.

1   2   3   4   5

b) I'm afraid that others—just about anyone—will find out how weak and unproductive I am.

1   2   3   4   5

c) I cause unpleasant scenes at home, which rapidly get out of control due to my anxiousness and frustrations.

1   2   3   4   5

d) I want everything my way; I make decisions quickly, and hate being second-guessed.

1   2   3   4   5

e) I try to keep a low profile at home as well as in social situations.

1   2   3   4   5

f) I bring work home in order to "finish it," and to start the next day without its burden, but end up never touching it.

1   2   3   4   5

TOTAL _____

4. a) I daydream about how it used to be.

1   2   3   4   5

b) I've been trying to hide at home in front of the television, behind the newspaper, and with alcohol.

1   2   3   4   5

c) My "avoidance level" has never been worse—I'm beginning to shut myself off from close family members and my spouse.

1   2   3   4   5

   d) Nobody really understands me, and how much work I
       do.

       1   2   3   4   5

   e) I trust no one; almost everyone is not worth my time.

       1   2   3   4   5

   f) By midday, I feel so stressed out that I know my job per-
      formance and productivity are nearly nonexistent.

       1   2   3   4   5

TOTAL _____

GRAND TOTAL _____

Once you've added up your points, if you've scored any-where between 80 and 105, you need to get some help. Reading this book is a good start; in the resources section at the back, I've listed additional places you should investigate.

If you're in the 50–80 zone, you may, unfortunately, be on your way to full-blown work addiction. Take a close look at where you scored highest; is it your anxiety about work? Is it your unhappiness with family, friends, and your social status? Does the higher number show you that your temper flares much too quickly, and that you may need some help in managing your anger? There are various components of workaholism, as this short quiz indicates. Anger and anxiety are the bedrock of this disease, and if you score high in those categories, you are headed for very unhappy and unproductive times.

If you scored between 26 and 50, you may be experiencing some day-to-day upsets or anxiousness that can be managed by being aware of what's causing the problem. You're doing okay now, but you may still be a candidate for the beast we're trying to tame.

It's important not to beat yourself up no matter how you score. This "assessment" is about getting better, not self-flagellation. If you scored high or in the warning area, the first thing you need to do is . . . nothing. Work teaches us to leap to fix the problem, to act quickly and efficiently and powerfully. That men are inveterate problem-solvers is as much of a cliché as the power lunch and the power tie, but the idea hasn't left our work culture. So your gut instinct, the one that made you a success at work, is to see the results of this quiz and "power" through to fix things. I don't know how many times I've said to myself, "If there is a problem, then there is a solution." We all talk about putting out fires. Well, this is one fire that has been burning for a long time. It's not going to hurt to let it burn a little longer.

Once you've discovered you have a problem with work, the first thing you need to decide is whether or not you're going to do something about it. That's the important decision to make.

What will hurt is trying for the quick fix. Workaholism isn't a hiccup in our lives, a flat tire that slows us down until we pop on a spare. Our problems with work have less to do with what we're doing but how and why. And so the solutions we need to find are deeper. The healing we need to find has to take place over a long period of time. It's more than a matter of saying to ourselves, "I have a problem with work, so this week I'm only going to work fifty hours instead of sixty or seventy." That won't work, because counting the number of hours doesn't address how we're spending them, or the way we're retreating from our family by leaving the cell phone on during dinner, or the anger we feel at a friend for not agreeing with us, when that's what we've come to expect from our underlings.

Now that you've taken the quiz, try to watch yourself during the day. The following chapters will help you see the patterns that you might have been missing. And once you educate yourself as to exactly what your problem is, getting help becomes much easier.

I used to have a joke that I'd use when I was caught red-handed doing too much—multitasking, spiraling out of control on work that should have been done, and, at the same time, getting crazed about the future: "I'll burn that bridge when I get to it."

Humor seems to help us with many problems (real and imagined), and I've found, at moments of panic, a joke, a laugh at oneself, puts a seemingly out-of-control situation back into perspective. Okay, you've got a problem, but it's not the end of the world. Ask yourself, Is this going to go before the entire United Nations Council? The last thing I want to leave you with at this stage is: Don't get into denial. It's like "one drink" is to an alcoholic. Admit your problem, decide you want to do something about it, and sit with that commitment for a while. If you feel the urge to blow it off—who wants to work at not being a workaholic?—look back at your quiz and remind yourself there's a better way. Or read on and see if what happened to me sounds uncomfortably familiar.

Chapter 3

Pulling the Trigger at Work

*The rung of a ladder was never meant to rest
upon, but only to hold a man's foot long enough
to enable him to put the other somewhat higher.*

—THOMAS HENRY HUXLEY,
"UP THE LADDER TO THE ROOF (AND THE LEDGE)"

Even if you've made the decision to strive for more balance
in your life, you can't move toward that goal without learning more about how you got to where you are in the first
place. You need to take a closer look at some of the unconscious assumptions you've made about why you "need" to
be the way you are. And you need to notice how you've set
up the little world of work around you to feed that part of
you that tries to live up to the standards you've set for
yourself.

Start by looking at the list of behaviors below. How many of these triggers apply to you?

The Triggers That Pull You Back

- You keep the computer on at home (assuming you keep your primary place of work elsewhere).
- You keep the computer on all the time.
- If you can access your office e-mail from home, you do so around the clock. It's not unusual for coworkers to get messages from you time-stamped late into the night or early in the morning.
- You answer those "last few calls" from your mobile phone. (The people who sit next to you on the train hate it, but that doesn't stop you.)
- You routinely give businesspeople and coworkers your home phone number (except, of course, in the case of real friends) and bless their full access ("Feel free to reach me anytime").
- You remove most of the contents from the top of your desk (including your "in basket") and all of your unanswered phone messages, and transport it all home. Because "you know you'll get it all done tonight." (Ever notice how many times the stuff just marinates overnight in your briefcase?)
- You offer to "take over a project," or help a coworker, even though you already have an enormous workload.
- You cancel out on a lot of social and family dates and obligations.

- You feel physically and psychologically drained before the day is over, but you keep at it anyway.
- You attempt to "look busy"—even though you should be, but your focus is off. You have no sense of priority.
- You get to the office before anyone else does. (And maybe you take some private glee in seeing that that e-mail to your supervisor is time-stamped well before 9:00 A.M.)
- You stay late enough to bid goodnight to the cleaning crew. (And maybe you get off on being an "hours queen," trying to outstay coworkers, privately believing that the ones who knock off before you are wimps.)
- You use your commute not to unwind but to "tie up loose ends."
- You check your pager and your watch constantly during social situations. Your cell phone is always clamped to your belt or handy in your pocket.
- You view an upcoming three-day weekend as a great time to catch up on work, rather than a great time to decompress.
- You call the office the minute your plane hits the tarmac while away on business (or pleasure).
- You grab a handful of antacids a little too often.
- You cancel doctor and dentist appointments and remake them in the future (only to cancel them again).
- You're afraid, although it's hard to say what you're afraid of.

Whether you're trying to conquer workaholism or are just recognizing that you suffer from it, it's important to learn what circumstances trigger your disease. If you've ever tried to quit smoking or go on a diet, you know how triggers work. It might be a cup of coffee or a gin and tonic that makes you crave that cigarette, or a bite of pasta that tempts you to break your diet by wolfing down a huge plateful of cannoli. The holidays are notorious for tripping all our triggers. There's the stress of family, the nostalgia for certain foods, the pressure from all around to indulge, to have that extra drink or that extra helping of food.

Work triggers function in the same way, and like the holidays, the things that feed off a workaholic's weaknesses are publicly sanctioned. Try telling the host of that holiday party that you've had enough to drink, or telling your mom you don't want any more turkey, and there is that brief moment of disappointment in their eyes. They might prod or cajole you, and most of the time you'll give in. The same thing happens at work, when faced with that extra bit of work a project needs, or the weekend call from your boss, or an out-of-town client who needs to be taken out to dinner when you'd rather go home to your family. This is how workaholism begins, with little fears and insecurities. Your boss asks you to stay late and you offer an excuse or some other kind of resistance, but then it's expected you'll eventually cave. After a while, these triggers morph into something else entirely, but they never go away. After a while, it doesn't take a "special" request from your boss for you to stay late. You do it yourself.

One of my biggest and most frequently battled triggers comes when a client asks, pleads, or begs for me to help them with something that is really not within my province. I am given to flattery, and my need for "importance" in people's lives can make me prone to overpromise and underdeliver.

What are your triggers? Start with the list above, and add the others that apply to you. Being aware of the triggers is the first step in learning not to trigger them.

Beyond the triggers lie larger issues. Many of us fall into workaholism because we're really trying to achieve other goals or fulfill what we perceive as needs. Let's take a closer look at the chief offenders.

Being a Good Provider

As we move into life, many of us decide to have children. As we add to our families, we do experience genuine joy. At least, at first. Then comes fear.

The realities of having the responsibility of raising a child force us to reconfigure our relationship to work. At the beginning, we tell ourselves that we can no longer spend endless hours at our desk, on the phone, or on a plane. The demands of these new people, and our partner, put a strain on our relationships, and an extra load on everyone.

Ironically, many of us begin our major retreat from the family not much after we *become* a family. As I'll discuss at length in the next chapter, our anxiety increases as we begin this abandonment, but we start to take refuge in our daily work routine. And who will call us on it? After all, "I'm providing for my family."

I know I started out working harder and harder to make my business succeed because I was watching my children grow up faster and faster. I felt a lot of pressure from all sides—from my wife, from my parents, from friends, and not least of all, from myself—to provide for them. Part of my worries were well founded. Making sure there is money for two kids to go to college is a legitimate worry, not to mention all the things children and families need or want right now. And a man doesn't have to be macho and sexist to want what's best for his family. Who hasn't looked up at the clock at quitting time and thought, "Maybe I should work a little bit longer, produce a little more today. Maybe that might help me get that raise." We all know those raises do add up to something tangible for our children.

Once you've had a certain amount of success providing, it's not as if you can stop. Families come to expect a certain standard of living, and that standard is a bar that's sure to be reset over time.

My family became used to expensive vacations, dining out frequently, living in large, beautiful homes, and possessing nearly every video game in nearly every format that existed. It wasn't that they asked for these things. In fact, they rarely, if ever, made requests for material goods. My providing them had almost entirely to do with my self-worth. I was heavily invested in being "the Great Provider."

In a dual-income family, the dirty little secret is that the one who gets the biggest paycheck is the one with the power. Both partners know it. Unless the assumption is challenged, the one who makes more money feels a greater sense of entitlement to decide how that money's spent. In most dual-income homes, Dad brings home the bigger paycheck, and it's a short hop to "Dad makes all the rules." It's really inevitable, unless, of course, both parties bring it out in the open, and talk about it without anger or remorse. It's hard not to get sucked into liking the feeling of being more powerful, of having more say, of getting your way most of the time. If "the man of the house" makes more money than his wife, it feeds directly into his need to work even more overtime, to make sure the balance of power continues to tip in his favor. He gets more and more lost in the labyrinth that is both his work and his refuge.

If we're such good providers, what are we providing for? Most of us would say that we're trying to reach our financial goals: putting the kids through college, saving up for retirement, and so forth. But take another look at where all that money is going; how much of it is spent buying off our loved ones and ourselves because we or they "deserve it"? Listen to Linda Kelley, author of *Two Incomes and Still Broke?*

We reward ourselves and spouses with unnecessary purchases because of the pressure and turmoil [of our jobs] and because we *deserve* it. We guilt buy for our children to replace the time we cannot give them and because they *deserve* it. When's the last time you came home from a business trip empty-handed? . . . Reward-guilt buys can also be contagious between family members. An overstressed worker rewards himself with ongoing purchases of new CDs to unwind during his commute home. His wife notices his growing collection and decides she has also earned the right to unwind and insists on ordering in pizza every Friday night. He sees the pizza as justification to buy a better CD player. She sees the CD player as evidence they can afford new carpet. . . . Keeping even on reward buys can turn into a cold war in which the buys might most honestly be labeled *get-even* buys. An "if you deserve that, then I deserve this" attitude can lead to more problems that threaten your marriage.

Whenever I get caught up in the image of myself as the Great Provider, I remember some wise advice from Suze Orman's *The 9 Steps to Financial Freedom:*

Pretend, for a while, that your house is a store. Walk around, and imagine that you were going to be putting a price tag on every item in this store. You know what you paid, when they were brand-new, for your sofa, refrigerator, washing machine, dining room table, dresser, and three-year-old car. What do you think they would be worth now? Affix the imaginary price tags to these items based on what they would be worth today if your life really were a store.

Now stop to examine the items that really matter to you, the items that resonate with meaning and memories, the items that tug at your heartstrings. Those tools your dad wanted you to have when he died. The funny lamp you and your first love bought when you fell in love and thought, in those days, that anything was possible. Your small daughter's stuffed animals, all lined up on a shelf. Family photos. A wedding ring. The painting over the mantel that was the first art you ever bought. . . . What kind of a price tag would you put on those items? What you're really asking is, What kind of a price tag can you put on your *life?*

The Need for Status

USA Today recently quoted the *Wirth Report*, which measured gender priorities for various goals. Here are the results:

- "Having a rewarding career": men dominate.
- "Achieving financial success": again, men dominate.

- "Developing personal relationships," i.e., friends: women dominate.
- Finding a "deeper purpose in life and growing spirituality": women dominate.

The list goes on, but without question, there are basic gender differences in what men and women want, admire, and strive for. But it isn't enough to look at gender-specific differences in attitude and desires. Women have ambition, just like men, but it's more often tempered by the need and desire to strike a balance between work and home life. We could learn from them.

Once a man has achieved some measure of success, the need to go beyond, to do better and better kicks in. While a man is on the upward path, things look bright and promising. He's on a roll. He needs more and more success. He needs to be envied, admired, perhaps even feared. The thirst that cannot be quenched is the terrible compulsion for a greater, higher, more esteemed perch in the workplace.

Many of us have experienced the high from the adrenaline rush on the way to the top. Did you peak yet? Why do you feel the need to do more, do your job better, smarter, and at the same time, why do you feel empty, without inner resolve and direction?

Alpha Male Behavior and Workaholism

Men who strive to get to the top—wherever that is—are bound to be workaholics. This is an arena where the hours put in at home don't count. Men don't reward one another for being great dads. Until very recently, paternity leave after the birth of a new family member was unheard of. Alpha males are the ones who perform on the job and who get their pack to perform. And the alpha male at work scrutinizes every other male's behavior and workload.

The only way to become the alpha male is to outperform the other contenders for the spot, to work harder, longer hours, and produce. It's a contest, it's a sport, and it's inhuman.

Does this colossal need to move upward leave you without emotional support?

Once you've had a taste of status, it's hard to go back. Money and status make everything so clear. We know what a Mercedes costs, and we know that other people know. Status symbols become a kind of shorthand for our self-worth. You need only look at the logo on the front of my car to know how much I'm worth. End of story. Nothing else in our lives, or those of our families and friends and children, works on such simple arithmetic. Real relationships with real people are complicated and messy and out of our control. They are consensual, full of give-and-take.

We cling to status because it doesn't ask anything back. As long as we can make the payment on that Mercedes, then it asks nothing more.

Fortunately, as a trigger, the need for status is more manageable than many, because as much pressure as there is from the outside world for us to be successful, most of the pressure comes from within. We can identify and fight our desires for material things, especially as we learn to find new ways of valuing ourselves.

The 24/7 Trigger

It would be easy to blame everything on today's workplace. When I think about how hard my father worked, how many meetings he held, phone calls he answered, letters he wrote and read, it seems almost laughably small compared to what people I know have to produce now. Businessmen today have some very real fears about the competition, because there really is someone out there who's willing to do it better, faster, and cheaper than you are. And so how are we supposed to respond? By ratcheting up the pace.

A lot of times it's right to blame work for making us toil too hard and too much. But are we responding to work honestly, or using the inherent pressures of a twenty-four-hour global workplace as an excuse to retreat into our work? That is the question we have to be aware of when we look at the pressures of the workplace as a trigger. Are we reacting to that phone call with a flurry of activity because it was truly urgent or because we want it to be urgent? I remember when a fax was the most urgent way of reaching someone. Then came FedEx, a great way of making something seem more important than it was. Then came e-mail and the Internet, thus removing any excuse anyone might have for not doing something *right now!* But how many times have you gotten that e-mail or fax or FedEx and realized that it could have waited? That bit of correspondence could have survived the three days it would have taken the post office to deliver it. Contrary to what we like to believe, most of the work we are doing is not that important, not that vital.

In his treatise on our society's increasing love affair with speed, *Faster: The Acceleration of Just About Everything*, science journalist James Gleick focuses on this phenomenon at work:

In a less connected time, any business deal based on an exchange of paperwork proceeded at a pace controlled by the mails—two, four, six, or more days between volleys. Then came universal overnight mail and its industrial-age children—in Federal Express jargon, "expedited cargo," "just-in-time delivery," "high-speed premium transportation," and "automating and streamlining the supply chain." Federal Express sold its services for "when it absolutely, positively has to be there overnight." In the world before FedEx, when "it" could not absolutely, positively be there overnight, it rarely had to. Now that it can, it must. Overnight mail, like so many of the hastening technologies, gave its first business customers a competitive edge. When everyone adopted overnight mail, equality was restored, and only the universally faster pace remained.

Like so many of us, I have an "in box" and an "out box." For a very long time, sometimes weeks at a time, I didn't get to the bottom of my "in box." I toted the contents back and forth from work, obsessed about it, worried as the pile got deeper and deeper. At the end of every day, I'd vow to get to the bottom of it, then beat myself up when I didn't. When I finally did clean the box out, down to the wire mesh, guess what I found? About 99 percent of the memos, reminders, newspaper and trade magazine clips were of no use—they had no bearing on what was current or important. They didn't have the slightest use for me whatsoever.

I won't deny that there were a couple of pieces of paper I should have read and dealt with weeks earlier, but so what? It'd be funny, except that I took my "in box" so seriously and let it loom so large in my life.

No matter how committed I am to breaking the habit, in order to hasten a business deal, or close one that's been lingering, I still find myself using the fax machine or e-mail more often than the phone—you can rarely get anyone to pick up right away. And, of course, I need an answer "right away."

Well, of course, I don't need it right away, and neither do you. Not unless you're in charge of a heart transplant. We need to get a little distance on what *is* urgent, and what *can* wait.

And let's also admit that we get off a little on the feeling of importance all this rush, rush, rush engenders. It's more confirmation that we matter; we're in the thick of things. As James Gleick puts it in *Faster:*

> We complain about our oversupply of information. We treasure it nonetheless. We aren't shutting down our E-mail addresses. On the contrary, we're buying pocket computers and cellular modems and mobile phones with tiny message screens to make sure that we can log in from the beaches and mountaintops. . . . The economist Herbert Stein, eyeing the new hordes of men and women who walk city sidewalks with cell phones at their ears and mouths, decided that our need for information on demand is as primitive an instinct as any animal can have: "It is the way of keeping contact with someone, anyone, who will reassure you that you are not alone. You may think you are checking on your portfolio, but deep down you are checking on your existence."

Perfectionism: Being Our Own Worst Enemy

Nothing I ever do is good enough. I don't know how many times I've thought this myself, or how many workaholics I've talked to who felt the same way. We who fall prey to this trigger don't need a boss to spur us on. Our own perfectionism is carrot and stick. How many times have you redrafted a proposal or a letter because it wasn't "quite right"? Or how many times have you finished a job and immediately started criticizing yourself for having done a mediocre job? And then, of course, you swear you'll do better the next time, that the next deal will be groundbreaking or the next sale will set the record.

The danger of this trigger is that it can be hard to recognize. After all, in order to do our jobs on their most basic level, we need to be able to judge our own work. The irony is that perfectionism distorts that judgment. When we fall victim to this trigger, we become convinced that if we don't do a perfect job, we'll be exposed as frauds, or reprimanded, or put at the back of the line. But who's watching us so closely? The answer, usually, is no one. We're the ones putting ourselves under such a hostile lens.

Perfectionism encourages the workaholic to work even harder—to achieve something that is both elusive and generally unattainable. Good work well done is never good enough for the perfectionist. Everything can be made to be better. That's the perfectionist's credo, but it's a myth.

We have to learn to accept a job done well. To accept the first draft of a letter. To agree not to overanalyze statements, financial or otherwise. Make a pact with yourself to befriend yourself, and agree to go easier on self-judgment. How many times have you consoled a friend or child, saying, "It's okay. Nobody's perfect"? Isn't it time you listened to your own advice?

Remember, nothing save for what we find in nature is "perfect." I've been listening more closely to praise from others—whether it's as a result of my work, or on a more personal level—and worrying less about my expectations.

The Invisible Man

When you become the one who hides—at home as well as in the work environment, causing pain and misunderstanding with family members as well as coworkers—you're close to bottoming out. You start to feel like a victim—of the demands of your work and your family. You haven't any more to give to just about anyone—certainly not yourself.

Your health begins to fail. You may start drinking or getting involved with drugs. Anything to mask the pain of the self-inflicted exile you now seek. Once the work alone would act as an anesthesia. And now work doesn't work anymore.

What fills the days and nights of a man who is in retreat?

- Emotional distancing and emotional neediness
- Depression
- Friendlessness
- Fighting phantom culprits
- Self-defeating behaviors
- Overeating
- Not eating enough
- Binge drinking
- Drug use
- Argumentativeness
- Sexual acting out and sexual anorexia
- Lack of personal interaction
- Keeping one's close family members at bay; general retreat
- Indiscriminate rage
- A sense of powerlessness

These are true danger signs—it would not be an exaggeration to submit to you that any and all of these may lead to premature death. If you exhibit six or seven of these behaviors in any pronounced way or in the long term, you most certainly are close to "bottoming out."

Some of you may read the above thoughts on triggers and have figured out how to start stopping yourself from falling victim to the common ones. Some of you may see those triggers as part of your past but find that your problems today have moved beyond that point. It's not the faxes and the boss and the pressure to succeed or the need for status. It's everything. *Everything* is hard; nothing makes sense. I reached that point, where even something as simple as getting dressed was nearly impossible. Even taking care of myself felt like work. And when it got to this point, I started feeling invisible.

Chapter 4

The Invisible Man Does His Disappearing Act

Turn back to the front of this book, where I've reprinted the lyrics to the Harry Chapin song "Cat's in the Cradle." Maybe you flipped right by this song and didn't even notice it. Maybe you glanced at the lyrics and remembered the period in the seventies when it played on an endless loop on every radio station. Like all the seventies fashions, hairstyles, books, and songs that may have seemed dead-on at the time, maybe it seems more cliché than anything else now. If the song is new to you, perhaps you read the words and thought, Well, I'm sure they thought it was deep at the time, but it's completely irrelevant now. I know that when I first heard that song, I thought, *"I'll never let that happen to me and my kids."* And how could it, given how I felt about my dad's workaholism? It happened. And not just because I passively allowed it. It happened because I was happily, willingly seduced by my own work narcissism. I became a walking cliché: the Great Provider Dad Who's Never There. The Invisible Man.

Granted, I had a great excuse at the beginning. With Wendy's decision to stay home with our first child, I was the only one bringing in any income. We needed it, with the mortgage and baby expenses and saving for Michael's future. Then Wendy and I started our new business, and like any new business, it needed attention 24/7 when we were getting it off the ground, and I gladly dove in to launch it into the stratosphere and then make sure it never lost altitude.

Meanwhile, as I mentioned, Wendy was doing 100 percent of the second shift. She'd help out at the office, then drag herself home to take care of a toddler and a newborn. On the weekends, I tried to help out, but Wendy was so inured to doing virtually everything that she took the momentum from the workweek right through the weekends. Laundry, feeding, changing—I was more than happy to let her move right into that.

The Widening Gulf

In her groundbreaking book *Kidding Ourselves: Breadwinning, Babies, and Bargaining Power,* Rhona Mahony, an attorney who specializes in helping women negotiate fair divisions of labor, discusses why it is that women end up so often with the lion's share of childcare, even when they consciously make attempts to encourage their husbands to do their fair share.

Mahony argues that one challenge is that our wives get a nine-month lead in emotional attachment to our kids. As excited as I was about becoming a father, I didn't have a fetus inside me turning and kicking to remind me of his presence. By nature, Wendy had a more powerful emotional attachment to our kids from the beginning. And she translated that attachment into parenting expertise far earlier than I did. Anything I could do, Wendy could do better. Mahony describes another couple whose experiences exactly paralleled our own:

> Jack loved his baby, but he hadn't already invested the months of effort and discomfort—the pregnancy—that gave Alice's feelings such urgency. Five minutes of listening to the baby wail and she would rush into its room to check the diaper. . . . Alice did not make use of the one thing that would have made Jack catch up with her in emotional attachment to the baby: stretches of solo time during which he was completely in charge of the baby. She had no intention of doing that because it was obvious to her that when it came to babies, men were complete knuckleheads. They shouldn't even try. Jack shared that belief. Thus, their childhood training, their attitudes, and their plans all meshed beautifully.

Once, though, when Alice was busy on the telephone, on the spur of the moment Jack changed a wet diaper. He folded the new diaper crookedly but effectively, caked the baby with powder, and put the wet diaper in the hamper. The baby cooed at him.

Not so tough, thought Jack.

When Alice got off the phone and went to the changing table, she shrieked. It looked like an explosion in a flour factory. The hamper lid was ajar. The baby was crawling toward it curiously.

Alice told Jack that he was an idiot, a slob, that the baby was about to drown in filthy diapers, that he'd just wasted two dollars worth of powder, and that the next time he got any bright ideas he should do her a favor and go sit in the cellar.

Jack didn't like it. The tender bud of experimentation, the first stirrings of self-confidence, the delicate dawn of realization that hands-on baby care had its own pleasures and rewards—all frozen out and buried as under an avalanche. Jack never again volunteered to change, dress, feed, or bathe any of his babies. . . . He had no clue that Jamie was allergic to wool, who Sally's best friend's babysitter was, or how to scramble an egg in such a way that Paula would consent to eat it. Successful child care equals the mastery of two million details, times the number of children, plus interaction effects for every possible combination of children. Jack didn't even know there was an equation.

My life as a father was just like Jack's. Wendy seemed to take to parenting almost effortlessly, to know just what to do. (Of course, I wasn't around for the countless hours she spent making mistakes, inventing solutions, practicing until she got it right, and generally investing the time it takes to learn the dizzying array of tasks that go into caring for babies and children.) I bumbled at everything, and Wendy would get exasperated when I tried to do it. Or I'd sit down to try to read the newspaper, and she'd announce that such-and-such had to be done right now. So I'd leap up to do it, then get criticized for doing it poorly. It was pretty powerful motivation for dropping out altogether. "Think you can do it better than me? Be my guest."

I didn't realize how we were perpetuating that traditional gulf between men and women on the path to becoming parents. Part of me subscribed to the mythology that mothers are naturally better nurturers, which I now think is untrue. I loved watching Wendy revel in her role as a mother, and she was so incredibly good at it. Her every move looked so natural; I felt awkward and incompetent. I never felt that way at work.

Part of me was relieved not to have to deal with all the poopy diapers, the boring routine of shoveling food into a baby's mouth, the tedious burping after feedings. It's hard to admit it, but there's so much about having children that's just plain boring. Changing the diapers over and over and over. Cleaning up the spills over and over and over. Who wants to be bored? At the end of a day of hard work at my office, I had something to show for it. At the end of a day with a baby, there can be nothing but a bursting diaper pail and a hamper full of outfit changes to show for it. I'm a results-oriented guy, and raising kids doesn't give you that kind of instant feedback. There's no report card.

Part of me was relieved to have a plausible excuse to relax when I got home. I was increasingly resentful that I had no time to myself. Every minute, it seemed, was spoken for. There wasn't a moment when someone didn't want something out of me. It frankly never occurred to me that Wendy might like time to herself—how exhausted she must have been doing all that double duty—because I believed she loved what she was doing. I think that kind of rationalization came pretty easily.

When Michael was born, I resented all the attention he needed and got. One of the reasons male workaholics so often have marital problems is that they allow, even actively encourage, their wives to become involved with the children to the exclusion of the husbands. There's a little simultaneous dance going on, and no one teaches you the steps. You're not available to her or the kids, so she becomes more unavailable to you, then she becomes more available to the children. You're left out more and more and more. A circle of ill feeling begins. I began to feel that I was a second-class citizen compared to the kids. I told myself I got only the crumbs off the table, emotionally and otherwise, while the kids got the very best of Wendy. Telling myself this made it easier for me to continue to distance myself.

I don't think I ever articulated it to myself, but I definitely felt a sense of entitlement. Why shouldn't I have more time to relax since I was working so hard? Unconsciously, I was buying into the idea that my work was the *real* work (read: the one that drew the paycheck) while Wendy's considerable efforts weren't the kind that warranted the nice sit-down with the newspaper and a drink I so richly deserved. Anyone who's ever spent a day in the company of a newborn knows what bullshit that is. Wendy was in fact working so much harder than I was, on so much less sleep, and getting hardly any acknowledgment from me for it. Later, a friend taught me the old rhyme that must have frozen the hearts of wives depending utterly on their husbands' largesse to keep the family together: "Clap hands, clap hands, 'cause Daddy is home. And Daddy has money and Mommy has none." I was the breadwinner who deserved his rest.

I now realize that I was cheating myself out of so much. I'm never going to argue that you'll find Nirvana in a dirty diaper, but I blew so many chances. I love my boys so much, but when they were little, I didn't really bond with them the way I should have. In truth, all the humdrum details were my opportunities to get to know them, to share more chuckles and smiles and stories.

Unconsciously, I was measuring my satisfaction with home life against my satisfaction on the job. That's really loading the dice. The real joy doesn't come from comparing the two; it's foolhardy to expect caring for infants and children to stack up to a fun drinks-and-dinner date with a client. The huge, rich rewards of parenting don't get parceled out on schedule; the investment of time in building a relationship with your child yields its results completely unpredictably over time. It isn't reasonable to compare it to the results-oriented arena of work, where the paychecks flow regularly, coworkers generally behave tidily (or at least don't weep uncontrollably and do exercise bowel control), and you usually know what you're doing.

Wave Bye-Bye to Daddy

One cost for not "being there" was missing some great moments as the kids grew up. I vowed to keep a book that would contain all the "funny" or "clever" things the kids would say when they were very young. I'd read them back at family gatherings; they'd become the running family jokes; Remember when . . . ? The book is empty. Not one note. How could there be any quotes, notes, or memories recorded, when I wasn't there?

Part of me knew I was missing a lot of the milestones—the first steps, first words, all the other firsts. But all too often as I was driving home, I'd picture the demands that would hit me the second I walked through the front door—screaming, crying, complaining—and my stomach would tighten with dread. (Why do we always hit each other with the problems first thing when we get home instead of the good stuff?) It was a relief to miss the Arsenic Hour, that horrible time of disintegration every parent knows. The kids are happy as clams in the afternoon, but as the dinner hour approaches, the baby's overstimulated and exhausted and cranky and begins to wail, sometimes crying for hours. The toddlers whine and fall apart. The house is chaos. I caught myself deliberately keeping my distance, creating busywork at the office to justify coming home later and later.

If the boys were asleep when I got home, I would make the appropriate noises—"Oh, gee, I missed reading the boys their bedtime stories again"—but truth to tell, sometimes it was just easier to come home to find the toys put away, the messes swept up, the boys bathed and in bed, where my chief duty was the fun stuff of tucking them in and kissing them goodnight. I was Daddy the White Knight, sweeping in to tell a funny story and share a hug, far above the frayed nerves and short tempers of the previous hours.

Sure, I'd come home and ask after the kids—"How was their day? What happened at school?" And it wasn't that I didn't listen with interest. I certainly cared. But not so much that it didn't all continue to pass me by.

From the beginning, Michael and Ross were a team, and Michael readily enlisted Ross in his own world. If he couldn't keep up in something, Michael would simply tutor him. I had no idea what miracles he was working. I came home one night when Ross was about two. He walked in with a book; I assumed he wanted me to read it to him. Instead, he calmly sat down and read it to me. Michael had taught him how to read, along with Wendy! I was thunderstruck; I'd had no idea this was going on. Obviously, it takes weeks and months to learn how to read, and I'd been so out of it that I had no idea what Ross was up to. Michael also had him doing math, multiplication on top of addition and subtraction, when he was still a toddler. "Michael taught Ross how to play chess? Wow, I can't believe it. He's only three. How can a three-year-old pick that up so quickly?"

Of course, it's not all wall-to-wall "good stuff" at home. The highlights are all mixed together with the routine stuff, so no alarm goes off at work that says, "get home ASAP; your thirteen-month-old daughter has learned to walk, or talk, or read, or dance, or play an instrument . . ."

Needless to say, Wendy was the parent who went to all the school gatherings, all the parent-teacher meetings. She'd bring back glowing reports, which obviously I basked in, but I was still missing the bigger picture. "You don't know what you're missing," she'd tell me. "You'd be so proud of the kids if you could just hear the teachers talking about them. It would be such a good thing for you to hear how well they're liked and how well they're doing from somebody else."

I tried to make it to at least some of the school plays and other events, but I could never give them my undivided attention. My mind would inevitably wander back to the office. "How should I prepare for that meeting tomorrow? Let me mentally draw up an agenda of points I want to make sure we cover. What's waiting for me to do at home? When is this thing going to be over so I can get back to work?" I'd be watching the boys sing Christmas carols or present their science fair projects, but I'd constantly be stealing glances at my watch: "When are we going to get out of here?" I'm embarrassed to admit that a few times I actually made Wendy go in a separate car so I could get home more quickly, as if I were such an important guy that I couldn't spare the ten minutes after the school event you typically spend milling around and chatting with the other parents while the kids gather up their things.

How many of us are absent for the "great stuff"—the "moments" that enrich our lives beyond all measure? You've got to be present, literally, physically, and emotionally, in order to enjoy what are the most fulfilling times parents can have. We cheat ourselves out of those times over and over, and, of course, they can never be recreated—video doesn't cut it.

The family quickly adapted to my being the Invisible Dad. They wore their routines into deep grooves. The three of them became a well-oiled machine, and I became the inevitable monkey wrench that brought things to a grinding halt. I'd come in on the three of them playing some game—"Hey, can I join in?"—and find that everyone would get annoyed by having to stop and explain the rules, correct my mistakes, and backtrack. Wendy would have let me come in and take over and read and play any time I wanted to, but I began to feel like an outsider.

Sometimes I'd walk in on them when Wendy was in the midst of putting the boys to bed. Any parent knows the importance of the nighttime routine. You get the kids cleaned up, in their pajamas, faces washed and teeth brushed. You calm them down with a book or some songs. They're practically falling asleep, they're so relaxed. Then in barges Dad, and suddenly the routine's interrupted. The kids are up and out of bed, all jazzed up, tiredness forgotten, and we'd have to do the whole routine again to get them back to bed. This at the end of another exhausting day for Wendy when she'd just been about to have a few quiet moments to herself. I felt like an intruder who'd spoiled the family's evening.

We all adopted unspoken assumptions and dynamics. "They're with their mother; they must be doing okay." In the beginning, I ceded most of the parenting to Wendy because I assumed she would always be the more competent one. Over time, with none of us challenging this assumption, it morphed into a kind of rule: Mom is the real parent; Mom's the one to go to for the important stuff. Of course, this just perpetuated the idea that I was a fifth wheel; they didn't need me to have fun. Ross was shockingly young when he figured out that he shouldn't demand too much of my time; he'd already understood that that was what Mom was for, horribly enough. The boys fell into their roles. If it's anything major, Mom'll take care of it. If you want to hop into a lap and act silly for a short period of time, go to Dad. I loved my time with the boys, but I always felt torn by this self-imposed pressure to break it up soon so I could get back to work. Or if I made the decision to blow off any work for a weekend to devote myself entirely to my family, I felt like I was making a major sacrifice rather than feeling entitled to the kind of work-free weekend most people take for granted.

The fact that I wasn't present for much of the kids' lives never stopped me from delivering the word from on high. I'm very solution oriented. Whenever there was a decision to be made, whether school related or day to day, I was the one who came up with the immediate answer and delivered it with great conviction, blissfully unaware of the subtle dynamics in relationships that go into any honest decision making in a family. Naturally, this undermined Wendy again and again, and it didn't teach the kids anything about the nature of making considered assessments.

I blew a real chance here. Raising kids is all about learning how to be patient. At the office, I prided myself on being a good listener; I enjoyed being thought of as an empathetic, thoughtful person. But I never learned how to really listen to my kids, to be patient with them, and I think that's carried through in their lives and in mine.

The Invisible Partner

During the whole time our kids were small, Wendy kept it up, working every shift, either on duty at the office or being CEO of our home. She, exhausted, but honestly happy, due to her dedication to raising the children, unknowingly allowed me to slip deeper into my disappearing act.

If she snapped at me because I wasn't doing something at home as well as she could, I told myself she was controlling, she didn't understand me. She worked hard to include me in the kids' lives, but we invested very little in strengthening our own relationship. She should have gotten more help from me. She deserved someone to share the good and the bad. She couldn't even share it in a conversation.

I'd drag myself home from work and just not have anything left for her. I'd make the small talk, but that's not enough to nurture a marriage. To her credit, Wendy never stopped trying to get me to open up. Why was I so invested elsewhere? Why couldn't I be more present for her and the kids? My first reaction was always to be totally defensive, to find fault with her, with the situation. I tried to tell her how overwhelmed I felt: "I have so much to do! What am I going to do?" Wendy would offer her support—"Maybe I can help you"—and I'd cut her off at the knees: "No, it'll take me longer to explain to you what needs to be done than just to do it myself." I thought Wendy was controlling, but this was really all about *my* God complex and control issues. I was so important, no one but me could solve my problems; I wouldn't even let Wendy share them.

Wives who have workaholics for husbands totally miss out on building a family with their partners. They end up creating what they can, supporting who they can, and resenting it all the while. Wendy and I lived in a home that was no refuge from work; ironically, we had helped create that hostile environment. Most women don't want to go to work and come home and go to work. Nor do men. But we can stretch our hours out, come home late, and have ready-made excuses partly because society protects us and partly because we know how to manipulate.

This is true: this year both my wife and I forgot our anniversary. If we hadn't gotten a greeting card in the mail from her sister, we'd have passed it by. Both of us are overextended for a range of reasons. How had we lost sight of each other? It wasn't always like that.

Our partners suffer the burden of our singular path. Wendy was subjected to a cold, unemotional man when she was hungry for a husband and lover who could communicate. She, too, retreated. Estranged from me, she began to limit herself to the necessary qualities of provider, nurturer, parent, and motivator, and to let those of wife and partner fall by the wayside. She suffered silently, because even if she could have told me what she needed and I could have understood it intellectually, it was my emotional side that would have had to react and reason with it.

Along with this Sahara of indifference, Wendy was not only forced to take on the role of both parents, she was shoehorned into the role of the perfectionist mom, which just made her feel more critical and controlling. She sought solace and support from the children. Confronted over and over by a husband who had emotionally abandoned her and the family, she began to question her own self-worth.

It's Safer at the Office

Home is often chaos, because that's real life. Kids don't follow any linear patterns of behavior; they're often irrational human beings. Men love linear patterns; give me point A, and I'll get you to point B. If I made a reasonable argument for something, I expected my kids to accept it; when they didn't, I'd be furious. One of the reasons I dreaded going home was that it was all up for grabs there. I didn't know what to expect, I never knew when someone was going to burst into tears or be deliriously happy. I could put tons of effort into something at home without any results guaranteed. It was all messy, human, real.

The fiction is at work, the fact is at home. I preferred the fiction.

And let's face it, not only were the rules at work clearer, but it was more intellectually stimulating. The better I got at it, the more it got my creative juices flowing. I could read an article in a magazine, call up the author, work up a book proposal, sell it at auction, and play a key role in creating a wonderful book. I could take a half-formed idea and work with an author to make it sparkle. I could match the right book ideas to the right editors. I could put together a creative deal for a book or movie. I could actually see my ideas taking concrete form.

A few months ago, I was talking with a friend who was raving about this weekend workshop he'd been in. He'd spent almost the entire Saturday with a client. They'd come up with this exciting new idea, they'd spent hours hammering out the basic plan, they hatched great new ways to package and market it. He'd been in his element; hours before, his ideas had just been floating around in the air, and suddenly they had this concrete product that was going to take on a life of its own. He loved his job, he loved how it brought his brain alive.

I was thrilled for him too; I knew just how he felt. It only occurred to me later that this guy was describing a precious weekend day away from his wife, his four-year-old daughter, and his newborn. I knew he was absolutely nuts about his family; he talked about them often with great pride. But had I ever seen him this excited about his daughter's first steps or words? How had his wife, who stayed at home and almost certainly was yearning for another set of helping hands and a break from the drudgery of childcare, felt about having him gone for half the weekend?

It's another real problem in trying to make home life stack up to the office. On your job, you're around other adults. When everything's working right, you're happy, you're stimulated, you're creative. You don't find too many people raving about the intellectual stimulation of childrearing. In fact, writer Anne Lamott, in *Operating Instructions*, a diary of her son's first year, famously described babies as taking some of mom's IQ points with them as they slide out the uterus. Anyone's who's spent any real time around kids knows that raising them is the biggest creative challenge you could ever have, but I wasn't seeing it that way. I was mostly seeing it as problems to be fixed.

And then, for some of us, the joys of home life don't hold a candle to the pure high adrenaline rush of working at top speed. Some of us are adrenaline junkies who, just as our physical workout/runner obsessive brothers feel compelled, do it for the altered state it brings to us. Landing the big author, cutting the big deal gave me the kind of addictive high I just couldn't get at home. I'd hug one of my sons and be flooded with how much I loved him and how much I loved this quiet moment—but put me in the office when I'm making the killer deal, and that kind of buzz would just sort of trump everything else.

How many times have you had to take a work call on the weekend and found yourself outwardly cursing the call to your spouse or family but feeling inwardly relieved? This is something you're really good at! I remember how I would hear the beep and hum of our home fax machine, a number we only gave out to our closest, most important clients, and I would pretend to be upset, only to run to it hoping it was something that I could work on right then. The hum of the fax told me I was important too.

So I let Wendy be great at the parenting; I'd be great at the breadwinning. I had all the more reason to be absent—and noble at the same time. I told myself that being at the ready for clients was an important part of becoming a successful businessman. I let that availability become an excuse to cut away from my family, friends, and spouse.

By definition, the further immersed we become in our jobs, the less we invest in anything outside of them. I became very one-track-minded about life. It centered around my career, and it left everything else out. My family became distractions, invaders, people to contend with. In my business, there's no way around having to read after hours. Piles of manuscripts lying around are a fact of life. The kids would walk in to ask a question or invite me to play, and I'd cut them off with, "Dad's got to read this; I can't talk to you right now. I can't play with you." It never seemed to occur to me that if an author had spent two or three years writing that novel, it wasn't reasonable of them to expect that I'd read it within forty-eight hours, but I felt the pressure to do so; they were important clients, and I was an important agent. The piles of manuscripts became a visible reminder in our house that while Dad was home in body, his spirit was back at the office.

It's an incredible revelation, to look back at the moments where your child or your spouse asked for some of your attention and realize that you looked at it not as a plea for your love but an interruption or intrusion. Was there anyone who didn't want a piece of me? There's no way I loved anyone more than Wendy, Michael, and Ross, so why was I so pissed off when they invaded my space when I had such important things to do? Every time I've had the epiphany that my family was what was really important, and I actually put down that manuscript or wrapped up that phone call, I would feel such a sense of rightness, that I was really getting it. So why was it so easy to fall right back into the rut of putting work first?

So much of this happens on an unconscious level. Ask most dads how they feel about their kids and their jobs, and they'll tell you how much they cherish the former and how they wish their jobs gave them more time with the kids. But then watch how they make unconscious choices that keep them from making that time. I know one guy who was negotiating with his wife to let him spend more weeknights taking potential clients out for drinks and dinner after work. Having a more prestigious client list would earn him a promotion and more money. He was also negotiating with her to have a third child. She'd raised the first two almost single-handedly because already he was spending so much time at his job, yet here he was telling her that he longed for another child yet simultaneously wanted to spend even more time away from the family! He honestly didn't see the contradictions in his case.

If you feel isolated, it's because, inadvertently or with forethought, you choose to be. It might take a long time and happen so gradually we are barely aware of it, but nonetheless, we choose to lose ourselves to the world at large. Our single-mindedness guides us, and our myopic views lead us to lose ourselves. But how much work is too much work? The perceived nobility that comes with throwing ourselves into our careers, and dedicating most of every day to our job, is terribly threatening to the core of humanity in each of us. This false dedication appears to most of us to be virtuous. In that way men are further reduced into "giving in"—allowing, and inviting their work to more wholly define them. Are there real rewards that come with the risks of this loss of self? As I've said, statistics indicate that productivity actually decreases the more overtime one is actively working. But we tell ourselves otherwise. We perpetuate our own misery better than anyone else. And in this case misery doesn't like—or need—company.

The Disappearing Friend

As I've said before, virtually all addictions, no matter what they are, ultimately make loners of their victims. Men who do too much—especially at work—don't have time for friends.

Oddly enough, long after we've been "public" about our dedication to our jobs, we begin to recede into ourselves. We don't have time to establish friendships, nor do we have the time or the inclination to keep up with old friends. Just as alcohol and drugs produce isolationists, so does work.

Anger and resentment begin to take hold. We may have created this world of work that has no doors or windows, but it still makes us angry, hurt, and alone.

And there is something ennobling about the lone wolf at work. So we feel some measure of comfort in that, and at the same time we think we've shed the need for friends. This isolationism leads to anxiety, worry, and even more avoidance of family and friends. We tend to obsess about work-related problems, focusing most, if not all, our psychic energy on things that do not engender and foster any relationships outside our work environment.

This is a self-perpetuating cycle. Workaholic behavior makes us far less appealing to others as potential friends. Our actions and our words say, "Stay Away," "Avoid at all Costs."

Friends learn to be tolerant of one another. Workaholics are not, by our nature, tolerant. Friends are good at trusting one another. Workaholics do not trust themselves, much less anyone else. Friends are accepting of one another. We accept nothing but performance, and it had better be the best you can possibly do. Friends are truthful with one another. Men who do too much don't have time to delve into "truthfulness"—we're far more apt to look for blame, and find excuses not to be emotionally accountable to others.

Work is our lover. Work is our haven. Work protects us from having to live a full life. It does not allow intimacy; it encourages deceitfulness (first, to ourselves, then to our friends and family members). Work does not permit relationships. It does foster bitterness, jealousness, backstabbing, rage, and misplaced ideas of revenge: "My boss criticized me for that last report, and I worked on it all weekend."

These reactions, behaviors, and negative inner voices are all liabilities, in any setting. They prevent any close relationships with others, cause friendships to errode, and families to be torn apart. Show me a man with no friends, and I'll show you a man who is a workaholic.

One by one, most of my close friends dropped out of sight. The daily phone calls became weekly, then monthly, then every few months; then we didn't even bother to call each other anymore. We'd send the holiday greeting cards and family newsletters, but there was no intimate contact. Forget about getting together; I was way too important and busy to do that. No movies, games, drinks, or dinner. I told myself, if I paused for a moment to dwell on it (which I rarely did), that my family was more important to me than my friends, and my time was limited, so I had to focus on the family. Of course, I wasn't doing that either; it was just another rationalization.

I lost touch with how important my friends could be as intimates and sounding boards, how much fun it was to talk about completely different kinds of stuff than what I discussed at home or at work. Friendship went from a need to a want to a kind of frill I could live without—or so I thought.

A Simmering Anger

I began to seek out more and more ways to be invisible—much like those children of alcoholics or drug addicts. I got away—any way I could. I avoided confrontation, no matter what kind or from whom. And it wasn't a conscious decision either. I became very self-involved and, ultimately, very self-centered. What work could I undertake in order not to be "found out"? Found out as what? As a fraud, as a person who was not in any way what he seemed to be. A person who could fake it in almost any environment. Hiding, or seeking some kind of refuge, is not just a male trait, but it's certainly common to men who hide behind, and in, their work.

What happens when we listen more closely for the phone than for the sound of our family's or friends' voices is that we get cut off from reality. We stop experiencing life as others know it. Emotionally adrift, we stop engaging in meaningful relationships. We begin to cut loose from those with whom we would normally share some intimacy. We lose the skills (and in many cases, the interest) to reach out to others. We no longer feel safe when asked to associate with others—whether it's with family, friends, or coworkers. We stop trusting our feelings or intuition. Occasionally, we will send messages that say "come and find me," but because we cannot sustain self-exposure and intimacy, this exercise becomes another way of abandoning our feelings and those with whom we have unrewarding relationships.

I developed a whole sulking routine when I felt like Wendy and the kids were excluding me. Sometimes I'd literally slip into a corner and look off into the distance, hurt and bewildered. I was certainly consciously trying to play the hurt party; what I wasn't conscious of was how stupid and childish I was being.

I was nursing an almost unrelenting anger. I felt a need for constant vigilance—I was always on the defensive. Always waiting for an attack. I'd force myself on the family, realize that they resented the intrusion, then lose my temper. Five minutes after I'd walked into the room intending to bond with my kids, I'd be raising my voice, getting all exercised. When the kids were at an age when by law they're supposed to be completely oppositional and irrational, I wouldn't see it as normal kid behavior but could barely contain my own temper, let alone help them deal with their own temper tantrums. When I realized that I couldn't really control my kids—as though that were a noble goal—I'd get really pissed off. They realized I was angry, but they never really understood what I was angry about; neither did I, really. I had a lot of indirect anger and hostility that no one in the family knew how to respond to because they didn't know where it came from. The kids were bewildered. I was sending the ultimate mixed message: Come get me; I want you—but stay where you are; I don't have time for you because I'm so busy.

Anger, especially misdirected, is a mainstay of the man

who has "crossed over" into workaholism. Because he has taken on so much, promised so much, he is self-burdened with enormous amounts of work and responsibilities. As I mentioned before, workaholics actually tend to be less productive, less creative, and in greater denial than ever. We see ourselves simultaneously as martyrs and as the ones in the right whose decisions should never be questioned. I've worked for workaholics and I'm a recovering one, too. I know how terrifying it is to be scrutinized by them, and how it must feel for others to be assessed by one.

What exactly are we angry about? Of course, we can vent at work, but we direct much of our fury at almost anything except work, because almost everything else behaves in an entirely different way. Our wives and our children don't care how efficiently we can analyze stock portfolios, or how savvy our deal-making skills are, or how good we are at meeting new clients, or coming up with brilliant marketing campaigns. These abilities may bring us great praise and great paychecks in the workplace, but at their heart they are impersonal skills. They don't mean much to someone who simply wants our time and attention.

So often we take our families for granted, as though they'll always be there when we want them. As the old saying goes, "You always hurt the ones you love"—it's so often true. We can lash out in nondirected anger, often irrational, at someone who is dependent on us; we wouldn't dare try something like that with the person (whoever it may be) who is actually the one who had caused our anger. Blow up at work and you could lose your job. Blow up at home, and they'll keep forgiving you: "Dad's so stressed out over work. He just needs his space."

The Downward Spiral

But once we've crossed over into workaholism, that's all we're good at, and we get angry when what we're good at at work isn't recognized at home. What the world wanted from me at work was rational and straightforward. I knew the job I needed to do, and it was a matter of how well I did it. But what my family wanted from me seemed completely random and irrational. And I was too deep in my work to understand that life as it should be lived can be random and irrational. That is the essence of emotional poverty: to be so empty of emotions, to be so devoid of feeling, you can't tell the difference between how life should be lived, and what merely needs to get done.

When I started to make mistakes in my work, forgetting important details, having to repeat tasks and be reminded of conversations I'd had, I became depressed, angry, and had an overwhelming feeling of self-defeat. All of this anger led to depression; I couldn't overcome a feeling of general malaise, of worthlessness. I could never do enough. I began to recognize that I'd failed our family. Now I suspected I was failing at work, as well. My emotional depression led to general inertia, and failure haunted me as persistently as a rain cloud over my head.

It was 1992. As I sat there at the kitchen table at 3:00 in the morning, I believed that I could never be happy. I had boxed myself into a corner. I'd worked so hard, been so successful, I'd given all I had, and yet I was completely miserable. And I believed that it was nobody else's problem but mine. I went upstairs and packed a suitcase. I left no note.

I didn't really know where I wanted to go. Irrationally, I just knew I needed to look for a place to live, to get away from home (from the very people who still cared), to find some refuge, a place with no mirrors and no memories. It didn't help that I had had too much to drink. Somehow I ended up at a hotel and spent the rest of the night sitting on the edge of the bed, trying to pull my thoughts into some kind of coherence.

I went from feeling sorry for myself to realizing, by daybreak, that I'd completely overreacted, that I was acting childish. I drove back to the house and fortunately got there before Wendy realized I had ever left.

It took a near-breakdown for me to get it. The way back was the way home.

Chapter 5

Waking Up with the House on Fire

There is no greater sin than enslavement to desire, no greater curse than discontent, no greater misfortune than selfish craving. Therefore, in being content, one will always have enough.

—LAO-TSU, *Tao Te Ching*

It's so simple, isn't it? Somewhere, whether it comes to us cerebrally, or from some other place where there's emotional truth, we know we are killing ourselves. But how do we stop aiding the drain when the force that tells us to self-destruct is so powerful?

I've told you about my own darkest moment. Your rock bottom may be different. Or, if you're lucky, you'll nip the problem of workaholism early on. Workaholism may be an insidious disease, but on the positive side, it doesn't come with the physical addictions of alcoholism and drug abuse (although there are side effects that include weight gain, weight loss, alcohol abuse, sexual promiscuity, and other obvious detrimental behaviors). This doesn't necessarily make it easier to cope with, but it can help, and when we're recovering from workaholism, we take all the help we can get.

After that horrible night at the kitchen table and hotel, I felt more alone than I'd ever felt in my entire life. I realized that while digging my own grave, I had no one, except my overburdened wife to lean on. I saw nothing remotely positive in my future. I felt emptiness and absolute despair. I didn't even want to see the sun rise.

I'd like to report that after this epiphany, I leapt up off that hotel bed and resolved to change then and there. Instead, I decided to vent more of the rage I had in surplus. I didn't suffer in silence. I found fault with everyone within sight. I decided that whatever had gone wrong, whatever hadn't turned out to my expectations, was always the responsibility of someone who let me down.

I went right back to the office and continued to burn the candle at both ends (hence waking up with the house on fire). I didn't want to face an extremely unhappy wife who felt alone in raising our children, overseeing the entire household, and living with an angry, overwhelmed, directionless man who was not "there" for her or, ultimately, for himself.

And then, horror of horrors, production began to slip at work. Ironically, even though virtually everything else had come crashing down on me, it was only when the business was beginning to falter that I finally began to come to my senses. I had been coasting for some time, based on the fact that we had had a very profitable period earlier in the year. Suddenly I had to accept that unless I pulled a rabbit out of a hat (and he'd better have an American Express Platinum card with him), we were desperately short on cash, and our receivables didn't look good, either. We were in danger of losing our house, and ever fearful of having my pride take a blow, I had to redouble my efforts to stay afloat.

Some small voice of reason inside me told me that I couldn't just work round the clock. I had to look for new clients, different sources of possible income; but I had to work smarter, not harder.

Now I was ready to listen to Wendy. It took the threat to my business for me to accept the threat to my home life. I knew that I had to make a change. But where would I start?

Preparing for Reentry

To change, of course, you need to want to change. You need to know what you're "reentering." You need to survey where you are, and where you want to go. It is not enough to say, "I have a bad cold, and I want to feel better," because workaholism leeches into virtually every part of our lives. My first step was to do nothing.

Step 1: Don't Just Do Something; Stand There

Because personal introspection is never in a workaholic man's agenda, it will be hard to begin looking within. But that is where you must begin. As I said earlier, you'll be tempted to jump in with both feet and solve the problem instantly. You can't. If you're coming back from total burnout, you need first to take time to do nothing. Don't plan anything. Get out of bed when you feel like it. Get dressed or don't. Watch TV or read the newspaper. Follow any impulse to be lazy and nonproductive you might have. Workaholism takes a physical as well as a mental toll, and you need to acknowledge it.

This is the time for self-(re)definition. Now is the time to be very much aware of how you proceed in life and in work. To some extent, you are amidst a substantial redefinition of your priorities in nearly every phase of your life. (I'll discuss this in more detail in Chapter 7.)

What you do with the work environment, as well as at home, must be done with full awareness of your status of a recovering workaholic. You cannot forget where you've been, any more than an alcoholic can neglect to pay attention to his sobriety on a daily basis. I'm not talking about becoming obsessed with your new life, but about integrating your new behaviors and awareness into your new life. You'll know when you may be falling back on old routines—and you'll be able to make your decisions with that awareness.

I have to admit that this was almost impossible for me to do. I'm a solutions guy, a problem solver. Wendy helped me realize that rushing headlong into getting better without self-reflection would be a Band-Aid, and I'd be setting myself up for relapse. Remember: it took you a long time to get here. Commit yourself to taking a long time to recover.

Step 2: Resolve to Get Help; Don't Go It Alone
Regardless of how you arrive at the idea that you need help, it always comes down to you. If, like me, you wake up with the house on fire, being confronted with nothing more than yourself and your addiction is a frightening, naked moment. Even before you begin your journey to healing, you must first confront yourself or what is left of it. And that confrontation is a scary prospect, especially for people like us who have hidden from such confrontations for so long.

And as we start our journey to healing, we must also realize that at first we are going to be alone in our battle. I didn't realize this when I started my road to recovery, but hopefully you can gain from my experience. Those first few days, weeks, and months can be very hard. There were times when I almost felt sicker getting better than I ever felt in the tightest grips of my disease. But you will heal if you let yourself. You will come out the other side. You're going to have to reach out to others like never before, and reach deep into yourself to find strength. And you'll find you have that strength, in greater quantities than imagined, and you'll find that support, because there are people out there who are waiting to help.

You may want to seek professional therapy or look for a Workaholics Anonymous group (you'll find more information on WA in Appendix A). Both of these avenues can give you a boost toward recognizing your work addiction and helping you take the first steps toward becoming alive again. How you make the journey is your choice.

In my case, my wife, ever the pillar of day-to-day stability in our family, helped to talk to me about how the quality (or lack of same) of our lives (the kids', too) had been affected by my disease. If you are lucky to have a close family member, a partner, or a close friend to be honest with you, and you're smart enough to listen, to truly absorb what is being said and asked of you, this communication could be your lifeline.

If you don't allow those voices in, you could totally bottom out, losing your job, your family, your self-esteem, even those precious material items you needed to prove yourself worthy. It's hard to ask for help, but you need to do it.

Step 3: Understand That You Have Choices

As a workaholic, you rarely, if ever, have thought about a world in which you had "choices." Even if you "loved" your job, it robbed you of a range of choices and balance. My friend Ben told me that he paradoxically felt freedom in his work. I asked him why. He said that at his job, he never had to make choices—he knew what had to be done, or someone told him what needed to be accomplished, and he merely complied.

I think what Ben related was really about the fear of engagement—if he had to become involved on any deeper level than he operated on, he would have to commit to a self-directed choice, which is born of some form of introspection. Ben's world of work gave him no choices (and no advancement, I might add), and he became comfortable, in his own way, with that arrangement.

When you believe you have choices, you will ultimately experience a great sense of freedom. However, the first wave of understanding that life is all about choice can be daunting and fill you with fear. If you admit that you have choices, it follows that you have to be responsible for those choices, which means you're responsible for the screw-ups as well as the triumphs. It's always more comfortable to have someone or someplace else to blame for your woes. Take a good look at the choices you make at work. You tell yourself, "I have to do this," and "I could never do that" because "they wouldn't like it," but how literally true is all that? Ultimately, your life is your choices.

I still have trouble remembering that I have choices in life. Maybe it's because I watched my father, chained to his desk day in and day out, and never realized until it was too late for me that he was doing this to himself—he held the jailer's key! And because when we reenter we still need to make a living, it's hard not to fall into the same patterns. We drive the same way to work, eat at the same handful of places for lunch, see the same circle of friends (if we haven't pushed them away) when the day is done. It doesn't seem like we have a lot of choices. When you recognize that you have the freedom to choose, you can start making real changes.

Don't confuse the power to choose with the power to control. Yes, we do control our lives, to a greater extent than we have ever thought, in that we can make choices. But autocratic control is an illusion; we have to let go of the goal that we can ever control things in that ultimate sense. Nor can we control the people around us. I really do not control my children—they will become who they are and what they've learned. Our goal here is to opt for the freedom of choice, not the tyranny of control.

Step 4: Repeat After Me: Each Day Is a New Day

It's true. This morning is not a continuation of last night, or the prior afternoon. It's important to recognize that the boundaries you begin to create will begin the healing process.

A personal daily inventory is another good tool in beginning this new life. What have you neglected in your world? What have you overlooked, shoved aside, ignored? Apart from your engagements with your partner, family members, and friends, what can you revisit that gives you a sincere sense of yourself? You now know that your work doesn't define you; you define your work, and now, your life.

It's hard to accept that you won't get better overnight. You're bound to slip up. If you start out with the mindset that each day is a new day, you'll be more accepting of those inevitable mistakes. You won't let a small relapse bloom into full-fledged workaholism. You'll be more patient with yourself.

Step 5: Acknowledge That You're Not Perfect

One of the first steps on the path to a healthier attitude about work includes acknowledging that you're not perfect; that no one is; that no one ever will be. It's like seeing the best-looking, most fit, most "together" man on the beach. Why measure yourself against him? What's the point? Do you know him to be perfect?

Acknowledge your strengths. Think about them. Don't get caught up in focusing on what you think are your shortcomings. That's what most of us do all day—that's one set of thoughts that got us into this situation in the first place. If you have that kind of inflexible thinking about yourself, certainly you have inflexible thought processes that are guardians in other aspects of your life. You're suffering because you were trying to be the perfect worker. Don't screw yourself by trying to be the perfect recoverer either.

It's hard not to be a perfectionist. I know; it's something I still struggle with. I have a great imagination. I can imagine that there is a perfect relationship; a perfect ballgame; a perfect room; a perfect job. Try as I will, and do, I still have that perfectionism gene that rears its ugly head from time to time. Perfectionists have to struggle because we've been negative for so long. When we were workaholics, we were the first to criticize, either ourselves or others. We developed an eagle eye for the shortcomings of others and ourselves. And the hardest part about not being a perfectionist, the part that rubs against our negative, know-it-all selves, is being able to say it's good enough. It's being able to look at a day's work and say, Enough. The proposal is good enough, the client is as happy as she is ever going to be. *Enough.* And while those might sound like harsh words, they aren't. They are liberating. There is great freedom and lightness in simply stopping and being happy with what you have. Don't be negative. Pessimism and cynicism are the real enemies.

I try to ask myself why I feel the way I do when I'm down and being judgmental. What's at the root of it? Can I change my reaction to negative behavior in others? Letting go to get your way—it may seem manipulative, and it is. But "letting go" is an act that keeps us at a distance from the frustrations of not being in control. (Control and perfectionism are joined at the hip.) "Getting my way," for me, means being more at ease and peaceful with the results of "letting go."

When I catch myself being highly judgmental or intractably opinionated, whatever talk or business is at hand has the better of me. I try to stop, examine the underpinnings of the "chain reaction" and, again, "let go."

It's not that I don't criticize myself. I do. But I don't live or die by minor mistakes I make, or by phone calls I forgot to return. The world continues to revolve around the sun without my help, and it always will. Some of my self-acceptance comes with age. It just does. You do get smarter. You know which fight to fight, and which ones aren't worth the time. But age isn't the only teacher. If you analyze the range of experiences you've had as a workaholic perfectionist, you begin to see repetitive behaviors: superhigh expectations . . . misplaced loyalties . . . trust in the wrong people . . . grandiosity . . . uncontrollable urges for more, more, more.

The urges toward perfectionism and control feed a bottomless appetite. Let them go.

Step 6: Reset Your Work Clock

The next thing you need to contemplate is how and when you will begin erecting new barriers and borders. Look at your workday—the eight-hour workday, not the old fifteen-hour workday. What really needs to be done?

Part of the twelve-step process is taking a fierce moral accounting of our shortcomings. We also need to take a fierce accounting of our careers. Start by writing down everything you do, everything you want to do, everything that is expected of you. And then once you've written it down, really think about it. What are the parts of the job that you overreact to? What are the parts of the job that can be eliminated? What parts don't need full attention? I found that when I made my list, I realized I was taking unimportant phone calls too seriously, flinching at every phone message but then answering it immediately. At the same time, I realized I was procrastinating on the calls that could lead to confrontation. Now I try to do the opposite. I know I can leave at five if I make the really tough callbacks. And I also know that a lot of the unimportant or less urgent calls can wait until tomorrow.

Being a clock-watcher isn't all bad. Being aware of the realities of the boundaries of time may help you, as it has me. I try to end my workday at 6:00 P.M. at the very latest, although I try to get out as close to 5:00 as I can. At first I was anxious about it. What if I didn't get the last phone call returned or send that last e-mail?

Ask yourself this: How much of a buzz are you getting from thinking that what you do is so important it can't wait until tomorrow? If it doesn't harm anyone, it certainly can.

Pace yourself during your workday. I used to have a burst of energy in the morning. By noon, I had written a plethora of letters, memos, and notes. I multitasked, which normally meant I made errors in spelling and word usage when I was writing and couldn't follow a phone conversation while writing away. I also routinely read and responded to e-mail while on the phone. I stopped this dual activity about the twentieth time the person I was on the phone asked, "Are you there?" or "Did you hear me?" This behavior isn't only unproductive, it's rude.

My afternoons were spent in a semiconscious state where, most of the time, I got little done. I became aware of how much "activity" I engineered and how little work actually got done. By the time evening rolled around, I was dead on my feet.

"Would you like to go out to dinner?" my wife would ask.

"No, I'm way too tired. I just want to come home and read."

Or

"How about a movie? We haven't seen a movie in months."

"Only an early movie. I'm too tired," I'd say, "to go to one after dinner."

You have the same clock on your wall that the rest of the world has. Why fight with it? Why dote on it? Create daily, weekly, monthly "time maps" for yourself. And don't make them impossible to follow. As a friend once said, "I am the cartographer for the road not taken."

Try this: Take a look at your calendar. Start with next

month—write 5:00 P.M. or even 6:00 P.M. (we have to go at this a little at a time) on two of the days of each week of that month. That notation means that the time you wrote is an appointment with yourself. You may not break it unless there exists a TRUE EMERGENCY (and you know what a true emergency is).

And if you don't, here are a few:

- A certain file that you had is missing and the business may lose a client if it's not recovered.
- The entire computer system crashed, and you're the only one who knows how to reboot it.
- The building exploded.

Not an Emergency:

- An unhappy client who is not key to the day-to-day success of the business demands your attention.
- The air conditioner has broken.
- The overnight package didn't show up at 10:30 A.M.
- The key to the men's room has been misplaced. (Believe it or not, I would get wrapped up in this kind of trivial nonsense all the time.)

This is time for you to go to the gym, take a walk, go to a movie, have a "date" with your partner, call a friend, revitalize a friendship that's been dormant. Catch up with siblings. Buy yourself a gift. Read every page of the Sports section (try to stay away from the Business section—that's a trigger if ever there was one).

Sometimes it's as simple as picking a day to quit at five no matter what. Or take the lead of a friend of mine, who has an arrangement worked out with his employer that in the summer he works a half day on Friday, no matter what. And that last phrase is the key. We need to learn to take time for what is important to us, no matter what.

Marking your calendar is an important symbol. It says, in writing, that what you've planned for outside your work is every bit as important as what you do at work. On my calendar, I've marked my "reading at home" days, days around the holidays so I can help Wendy get ready for them. I take the school calendar, find out when the kids' breaks are, and put them right into my own calendar. Sometimes I'm planning six to ten months ahead to block those days off for my family. My assistants know that those days are sacrosanct, that those appointments are unbreakable. We plan around them, not vice versa.

When I first started marking up my calendar, I didn't treat the appointments with myself, friends, or family seriously enough. I'd mark off a day to go to the gym, then get there at 5:30 or 6:00 when it was a mob scene, and get discouraged. So I retimed my departure to get to the gym when it was less crowded and I could enjoy the experience.

Now I go four nights a week and feel great about it. Feeling more fit gives me more energy, which increases my motivation to stick to it.

In a recent article in the *New York Times*, Lisa Belkin reported on a newlywed man's promise to himself to take his new wife out to lunch at least twice a month. They'd found themselves so caught up in their lives and after-work plans with others that they barely saw each other during the week, and then were generally too tired to make much of an effort to communicate. The man decided that a good solution would be to make time in the middle of the day to connect with his wife. He confided his plan to a colleague, a marriage veteran, who freely admitted to adoring his wife and child but laughed off the plan, arguing that reality would inevitably intrude. The vet predicted that the couple would end up canceling or postponing their lunch date over and over despite their good intentions once they got caught up in the whirl of their work-days. The two men decided to raise the stakes: the skeptical vet would pay the newlywed $100 for every lunch date he kept with his wife beyond the twice-monthly minimum, and the newlywed would pony up $100 for every lunch below that minimum.

The jury's still out on who's going to collect here, but I really admire the principle. First, here's a guy who's staking a claim in the middle of the workday to connect with someone he loves; you could just as easily commit that time to meet regularly with a friend or with a group. Second, to increase his motivation, he's announcing his plan to someone else, and even putting some money on the line to increase the chances that he'll keep his priorities straight. We've all seen that wonderful *New Yorker* cartoon where one harried executive is frantically paging through his datebook, trying to find a mutually satisfactory date to set up a meeting with a colleague. He's barking into the phone, "How about never? Is never good for you?" The point here is that if we don't reclaim this time as our own and set concrete plans to use it, we'll let another lunch hour whiz by at our desks. We'll have stuffed in some food we probably won't even remember eating and missed the chance to lift our heads out of our jobs and take a break.

Use that lunch hour. Get yourself away from work. It doesn't have to be about food—I'm a big fan of a pleasant stroll around the neighborhood—but your lunch hour should be about connecting to the world outside work, preferably with other people.

It's Friday evening. Are you stuffing a briefcase or book-bag with stuff to take home "so you can catch up"? Or are you making plans to stop back in at work "for just an hour or two" over the weekend to "clear up some loose ends"? I've got news for you. If you're like most working folks, you're never going to catch up completely, and you're always going to have some loose ends fraying around you. Your challenge should be not to try to win this losing battle but to learn to live with the feeling that *it didn't all get done and that's okay*. Wanting to be on top of everything is just another disguise for the trap of perfectionism.

I remember reading a few years ago about how the Japanese government was offering cash incentives to employees to make them take off weekends and vacations; the government wanted to cut overtime and encourage workers to spread more of their money around the economy through tourism, shopping, etc. I put down that article and thought, "How pathetic are these people?" And then I realized that I wasn't all that different. I rarely took weekends off, and if I did, I felt guilty.

Not any more. Unless there's some dire emergency, I do my best to dedicate my weekends to everything but work. Mostly, they're about my family, my hobbies, and other outside interests. It's a chance for me to recharge my batteries, step away from the fray, and get different parts of my brain working. When I get back to work Monday, I honestly believe I'm more creative and productive for having taken that break.

Start reclaiming your weekends. Make it a rule not to set foot in the office then, and don't tempt yourself by bringing work home or obsessively checking your phone and e-mail messages. It can all wait. Everything will spin nicely without you, whether you like that thought or not, and your family and friends need and want you more.

I know, this is easier said than done, especially if your trigger is seeing the weekend as a really great chance to "get a lot done." But make a commitment to yourself to give yourself this two-day break every week, no matter what. I promise you, you'll be a better worker and a better person.

Step 7: Start Small

When you attempt to make changes, don't take too big a bite. Start by leaving work at an appointed hour. Then move into taking breaks—even leaving the work premises for that break. Then reclaim lunch. Leave work at your workstation—don't stuff it in a file or briefcase and take it home. If you can't reclaim your whole weekend, aim for at least one whole day off, with an eye to expanding those hours of freedom.

Don't overpromise. Don't raise your hand every time the boss asks for a volunteer. See a friend (or cultivate one) during lunch and do it out of the office. Plan vacations and don't take work or a cell phone with you. Entrust coworkers with your home phone only for true emergencies.

Go to a ball game. Buy season tickets. See a movie. Pick out a couple of books you've wanted to read . . . and read them. Add pleasure to your day. Little by little you'll be able to integrate these leisure activities into your life. As you do, reacquaint yourself with your spouse, partner, friends, and family (I'll discuss this further in Chapter 7). Don't overcommit to them—that's another trade-off for workaholism. Attempt balance. It will come if you let it.

Make every footfall your own. Don't rely on what you remember you "should" say. Begin to say what you want to say, think, feel, remember, believe, love, create.

The mistake people make is in thinking that we need to make big changes to affect our lives. But it's the little changes that matter, the small choices that send ripples through our lives. I quit smoking many years ago, quit cold turkey from a four-pack-a-day habit. And even though my life isn't radically different, it's different enough that I'm grateful for making that small change.

Just giving up and fighting against our workaholism is a big enough change. Don't burden yourself with bigger changes right away. Keep it small. Make a list of friends you've fallen out of touch with, and make a commitment to get back in touch with one of them. Maybe you'll only call once a month or send an e-mail or two, but rekindling that old friendship will start to mean something to you. It will start to have a value to you that work can never have.

And that's what we're trying to do when we reenter the world: we're trying to find or reclaim our values. It's a word that gets bandied about in the political arena, but I'm not talking about society's values, rather yours as an individual. And those values don't have to be an anything high-minded. You might choose simply to value friendship over work, or contemplation over action, or peace over hurriedness. You will find what your own values are when you start coping with your workaholism. And those values will give you the strength to succeed in your efforts. Finding and fighting for those values will ultimately be self-fulfilling and freeing, and lead to a richer, less complicated and fearful life.

Step by step. Real change comes gradually; forced change most often ends up in failure.

Step 8: Stay Positive

Begin to think more positively than you have in the past. Take note: What have I done that's positive? What would I do, what do I want to do, that's positive? Don't be afraid to ask these questions. In the words of bestselling author of *Codependent No More*, Melody Beattie, "Stop being mean to yourself." Being optimistic and positive is a struggle. When we were working sixty, seventy, eighty hours a week, striving, pushing, living aggressively, we came to think that people who went home at 5:00 were fools (or losers). These were signs of weakness, of being a Pollyanna. We trained ourselves to think that there was virtue in being ever-negative, ever-vigilant: everything was not all right, the roof was caving in. Our default mode was "putting out fires"; we need to combat that attitude. Fires are serious, fires burn. And unless we're conducting emergency heart surgery, most of what we do is not as serious as we think. Which is why being positive is so important.

Step 9: Make Time to Develop New Energies,
New Interests

Allow yourself to return to the true joys in life—whether they come in the form of a rebirth of the family, a new and intimate relationship, or the freedom you feel by joining a gym, a church group, or just about anything that you've left out in the name of work and productivity.

But don't rush to fill the time you've now created. Enjoy the empty spaces. Do something only if it brings you joy. Listen for that whisper of guilt that tells you you're "wasting time" in your new pursuits and extinguish it.

Workaholics feel claustrophobic mentally, emotionally, and sometimes physically. Taking joy in a new sense of well-being and "aliveness" breaks down the walls. As we begin to forgive and forget past offenses (real or imagined) and feel truly comfortable in our new lives, each day is easier, clearer, full of the praise of the unexpected.

Take your time.

Chapter 6

Making the World of Work Work for You

If we take the right steps, we will get better, but the world won't necessarily heal along with us. There is still a world out there filled with faxes and e-mails and urgent phone calls, but even more, that world is filled with attitudes about work that aren't going to change just because you want to or need to.

The Work Ethic

"The Puritan Work Ethic." Or just "the Work Ethic." However you say it, or claim its derivation, it means one thing: the more I work, the better a person I am. The tools and mottoes surround you; you can't get away from the visual reminder or the haunting internal voice telling you that virtue = work:

Telephones

FedEx's

Faxes

Cell phones

Car phones

Palm Pilots

E-mail

Laptops

"Idle hands are the devil's workshop."

"This is my life's work."

"An honest day's work."

"I need it now."

"Where have you been?"

"Just do it!"

"I'll do it myself!"

Never has there been a time when workaholics are so well rewarded, and so easily "made." With IBM, Microsoft, Motorola, Apple, and all the rest of the new machines that make information immediate, it's a quick slide from doing 100 percent of your work away from home to taking it all home. Or into the car. Or on the walk from the car to the office. And on and on . . .

Begin to look at others—your coworkers, your boss, your support staff—through new eyes. You spend more time with these people than with friends and family. Take some time to feel and think about their jobs. Do they seem totally fulfilled? Is the workplace their only world? Do they have "other lives"—families, friends, lovers? How have you been feeding off the energy of this atmosphere? If you're in a place that values workaholism more than balance, it's hard to fight the infection. If you've only ever thought about your coworkers in terms of what they've achieved, now's the time to start appraising them for the other parts of their lives. If you don't like what you see, why are you working so hard to emulate them?

Erma Bombeck wrote a very moving tribute to her father after his death:

> I went to my room and felt under the bed for the father doll. When I found him, I dusted him off and put him on my bed. He never did anything. I didn't know his leaving would hurt so much. I still don't know why.

And Colman McCarthy echoed the sentiment:

> Our fathers provided everything we ever wanted, except, of course, himself. . . . The workaholic, plagued though he be, is unlikely to change. Why? Because he is a sort of paragon of virtue. He is chosen as the most likely to succeed.

One fire fueling another. Who doesn't want to be virtuous?

No matter where you are in your workaholism, you cannot change the world around you. And the world believes in work. Ever sit on a plane and count how many passengers are working on laptops, going through their mail, or clearly working from their briefcases? We don't even allow ourselves the downtime of gazing at the clouds at thirty-five thousand feet; we're annoyed when the pilot tells us we have to "turn off all electronic devices" until further notice, as if those fifteen minutes were so crucial.

We can learn to spot and challenge the triggers at work, but what about the workplace as an environment? We can't stop working just because we're workaholics, but we also can't ignore what the workplace can do to us.

Neo-Puritanism

A wave of fundamentalist reactions is sweeping the country now. We seem to be overreacting to several decades of decadence—from a personal lack of moral or ethical behaviors to seeing our onetime heroes in sports, government, and entertainment get away with murder, in some cases literally. While there is a lot of good coming out of people wanting to live "cleaner" lives, there is also danger. People who used to throw themselves into drinking or drugs or sex are now throwing themselves just as violently into work and exercise. These people are still acting like addicts, but now the object of their addiction is okay because you can never be too rich or too thin. They've traded their cocktails for cell phones. And the workplace not only sanctions workaholism, it outright encourages it.

Obviously, the solution isn't to go back into the party-hardy addictions of the eighties and nineties but to recognize how infectious the new addiction to work has become. Even if you aren't one of those people rebounding from substance abuse or recovering from another addiction, you can still pick up on the overall atmosphere of today, in which people demonize past excesses but sanction current "virtuous" ones. You can still hide in your pursuits no matter what they are. The key is to make sure that you're doing things for the right reason.

"If You Don't Come in on Sunday, Don't Bother to Come in on Monday."

Yes, that's a quote. Not urban legend. It's attributable to a very well known Hollywood executive who, like most alpha males, expects total allegiance and obsession from his staff members.

Of course, like all good workaholics, at one time I not only would have understood a boss who expected total career immersion, I would have followed right along.

We need to learn to take time for what is important to us, no matter what. And this can be the hardest thing to let go of when we start fighting our workaholism. One of our fears has always been that if we don't do something, someone else will, and that someone (whom we perceive as younger, more talented, in better with the boss) will leapfrog us and take our glory.

Let them.

When I first stopped listening for the other Players snapping at my heels, it was hard as hell not to turn right around and hole myself up back in my office. Gradually, it dawned on me that my family still loved me. My health was still good. I knew I wouldn't be in line to prove myself all over again. I wouldn't let my head be on that particular chopping block. I might have had a fool for a boss for some years, but he's gotten much better, and much wiser.

When we're serious about getting better, we are serious about our time. We're ready to stop playing around, to stop rescheduling family time, and cutting short vacations, and leaving in the middle of dinner. And if someone else wants to live that life, that sick, lonely isolated life we're trying to leave, if someone else wants to work eighty hours a week, then let them. We know what it's like to be sick. They can have it.

Please Please Me

Workaholics are pleasers. It may not seem so on the surface (when we're on overload, we tend to be quick to temper, generally irritable, and often downright antisocial), but we inherited the need to please from our fathers, whose workaholism we have imitated. Often, we are also perfectionists, finding that nothing meets our high standards and expectations.

With the extreme increase in the pace at which we work, workaholism is bred in the workplace. As the bar continues to be raised, virtually no one can perform up to what is demanded. It is now demanded of us that we become pleasers in order to survive. Put all those e-mails, faxes, phone calls, regular mail, and overnight deliveries together, and you have a petri dish just waiting for a man with all the right addictive receptors to be infected by the new work environment.

But just as we reminded ourselves that all the old adages about hard work aren't always true, we can train ourselves to be less eager to meet the demands of the new workplace. It's a fine line to walk, but with practice it can make sense. The first thing we need to do is identify what's important at work and what isn't. This isn't always easy, especially in the high-tech workplace, where every bit of correspondence seems to be marked urgent.

Work for work's sake. You know it when you see it, or are asked to do it. Try not to get bogged down in senseless activity. Pace yourself. Don't let someone else impose his or her pace on you. Your work will suffer, and so will you. On the other hand, working at your own pace will doubtless allow you to do a superior job.

You may want to take a time management class or read a book on the subject to learn how to prioritize; or you may simply want to pick one thing that makes you jump and change how you deal with it. Maybe give yourself two hours to respond to a fax or wait a half hour after receiving an e-mail before you open it. And what do you find when you start fighting your urge to please? That most of the time the world doesn't even notice.

In *Change Your Brain, Change Your Life*, clinical neuro-scientist Daniel G. Amen, M.D., offers a simple prescription for his patients who spend too much time worrying about what other people think of them. He teaches them the "18/40/60 Rule":

- When you're eighteen, you worry about what everybody is thinking of you.
- When you're forty, you don't give a damn about what anybody thinks of you.
- When you're sixty, you realize nobody's been thinking about you at all.

That's the crux of it; so much of our drive to work too much is driven by the desire to please phantoms. Our colleagues want our strong efforts, but they don't want us rendering flesh and bone to them.

I'm not encouraging you to do a shoddy job, or make only a passing attempt at work. But let's face it, if you were hit by a car in the parking lot this afternoon, would the entire business fold, go bankrupt, would the building burn down? No. A job well done should be rewarded; a job done to death ought not to be.

Saying No on the Job

"I can't keep up" says a man I know. "There's no way. When I'm running on all cylinders, I'm forced to do a mediocre job, and my clients know it, and so does my boss." But rather than stand up to his supervisor, this man subscribes to the theory that it's better to do a mediocre job while being on duty 24/7 than to take a break and give the appearance that you're anything less than 100 percent committed to your work.

There is danger in this kind of thinking. Like the perfectionism trigger we discussed in the last chapter, sometimes we get the worst of it from ourselves. And one of the hardest things about workaholism is figuring out how to take the criticism of others. In this case, my friend's boss is as swamped as he is. A lot of what he is doing is taking her comments and amplifying and personalizing them.

Workaholism is not only rampant, it's communicable. The demands our supervisors put on us are often unrealistic. What we promise to do and the reality of what we *can* do often don't match.

"I don't want to work as hard as my boss does," another friend tells me. "She doesn't have a family; I do. She's just gotten her MBA, and thinks she knows everything. She wants to initiate new systems and analyze everything. Our whole department is being tyrannized by her need to fill her life with work. We're supposed to be excited and appropriately challenged by all the new technologies and information systems. Instead, I find myself falling back and using the library's stacks and special requests desks. And I feel like I've failed nearly every day."

Where's the real failure here? In the worker or in the system? We need to understand that each of us cannot control, change, or obliterate most of the things that cause stress. But until we can remove ourselves from them and set boundaries around time spent at our work, it's hard to fully grasp how little control we have and how powerful the outside world is. Sometimes even the smallest bit of bad news is enough to send us reeling.

"The mind's interpretation of an event is a way that causes characteristic physical effects," says Dr. Phillip Eichling, medical director of the famous Canyon Ranch spa. "You cannot control outside stressors, but you can control how you perceive and react to those stressors."

You don't have to beat yourself up because you think you're letting your boss down. You can step back and try to assess the situation. Is what's being asked of you realistic? Would you ask it of someone else? Instead of silently accepting the status quo, you can try to communicate your reality to your supervisor. Let him or her in on what your priorities are, and your self-expectations. If you are being tyrannized and the demands that are being made of you are out of hand, don't spiral out and get into self-blame. Just because your boss's house is on fire, doesn't mean you lit the match.

Try reasoning with your boss. Let him or her know you want to do a good job—and you intend to. But you also have a life outside of the office, which, you may gently point out to him or her (and yourself), has made you a more thoughtful and productive worker. You are not just your work; your identity is comprised of so many components—perhaps your love for music, poetry, football, cars, your partner. Your boss needs to understand that these are not just "interruptions" in your work—they are part of the tapestry of who you are. And who you are is why you were hired in the first place.

Too many managers have their priorities all screwed up. I honestly believe that you get a greal deal more productivity from people if you treat them like adults instead of hired hands, if you show your employees mutual respect and take a genuine interest in them as human beings.

We work in a highly stressful, social business. I like to see people who work with me happy, and the less stress there is, the happier and more productive they are. So we take half days off on Friday during the summer. I encourage my employees to go home at a reasonable time. To go out during the day and get some sun and some air.

I fully expect one of our young men in the office to take paternity leave when his wife has their baby. It's humane. It's appropriate. It's about life and balance.

I actually find myself (mildly) admonishing a coworker who works too many hours, or comes in on weekends. If there's an emergency, then fine, but that should never be the norm. I'm conscious of the fact that as a recovering workaholic, I want to model better behavior for the people who work for me.

If you can say to your superior, "If I take this project on, it may not get done on time because I'm steeped in A, B, and C," you're way ahead of the game.

Another way to appeal to your boss is to say, "I want to do a really good job at this, but I fear that I've got too much to juggle, and doing all of this may create a situation where my work is less than satisfactory to me and, ultimately, to you." Or you can argue, "I'll be more productive for you if you allow me to leave two afternoons early to pick up my daughter at daycare. I'll be a better, happier person, and you'll see better job performance." Before I found the courage to work for myself, I had to work up the courage to ask my old supervisors, "Do you want it now, or do you want it good?" Today this is a question I want all my employees to ask of themselves.

This is not just about manipulation. You're not trying to get out of work or responsibility. If you offer a trade-off, say leaving early to pick up your daughter in exchange for higher productivity, you've got to honor that promise. The magic of it is that it's true; being happier *will* make you more productive. It's about reason. One fireman cannot put out the fires on an entire block's worth of houses.

I'd much prefer the people who work for me to tell me they're stressed out, on overload, and their work is suffering, than keep piling more and more work on them. What's the point?

We can't buck the reality of the workplace; we really are expected to do more in less time, to give each project less individual attention so we can work our way through more of them. I'm seeing more and more managers understanding that the way to get the best out of their employees is to encourage more flexibility. But if your boss is totally impervious to your reasoned arguments, if he or she has no discernible humanity to which you can appeal, let's face it: you're in the wrong place anyway. It's easy for me to say, but you'd better find a way out of there, because you're going to go down with that supervisor; he or she is going to make sure you do. If you stick with a job that doesn't encourage you to nurture what's most important to you,

you'll end up only being a gear in the whole mechanism your boss wants turned out. If you want to be a gear that never needs any oil and attention, you're missing out on the chance for a more exciting, challenging, fulfilling career. You're turning into a drone.

You can also learn to ignore some of the broader assumptions about work. When a coworker praises you for a job well done, you can still enjoy the compliment, but you can also remind yourself that there is more to life than "good job." Or maybe the next time you're encouraged to "look busy" because an important client is coming over, you can choose not to, if only because you understand that looking busy, or even being busy, doesn't necessarily mean you're living at your best.

You want to love your job; you just don't want to be a slave to it. Finding balance outside of work will make you a better worker, someone who can bring a fresher perspective to the job.

Learning from Generations X and Y

The pendulum is now swinging in the opposite direction. There's a whole new generation of people in their twenties and thirties who are looking beyond traditional jobs and challenging the paradigm for the long-term loyalties that the generations ahead of them valued. This is not to suggest that all young adults make a habit of moving from job to job or that they lack focus and direction. It does, however, suggest that such direction is subject to the winds of change, which are now coming at hurricane force. Looking at life in a new way, these young people are experimenting with new relationships to work. The changes that permeate their world of work are a reflection of the technological society in which they live. It's not easy to find a career that is fulfilling while subject to daily change. I'm seeing lots of younger adults searching for careers that allow flexibility but don't inhibit their growth or outside interests.

A few years ago, Gen X "slackers" were a popular topic, those twenty-something youths who were eschewing corporate life and living their days out in coffee shops and nightclubs. Sounds good to me. I can think of no better way of spending your youth than wasting it. And if you think you disagree, how many times have you thought back to your college days and wished for those simpler times? I'm all for more of us doing more slacking. Unfortunately, a lot of the young people in today's turbo-charged economy aren't spending their twenties aimlessly traveling or writing bad poetry. They are entrepreneurs at eighteen, something that many older people wouldn't have dreamed of trying until they had much more work and life experience. As exciting as it is to see them achieve so much at so young an age (although the paranoid side of me admits that it's one more incentive to put my nose back to the grindstone), I worry that they're cultivating the joys of workaholism at too tender an age.

On the other hand, I'm seeing a new group of entrepreneurs who may be starting "dot-coms" or other new ventures, but who are making their work an integrated part of their "whole" lives. I think they're onto something much healthier than I was at their age. Start-ups these days seem to have a more casual atmosphere, one in which formality and pecking order are nearly nonexistent. Structured more like an extended family, these businesses seem to think with more of a collegial attitude, one that says "we're in this together." It's less adversarial, more community driven. Doors are open, workspaces less fortresslike. Rigidity has been replaced by flexibility. A genuine caring atmosphere is bred more exactly in these new places of work. Workers may share space and trade hours. Many people work from home. There's a lot in this new model of work to emulate.

On the Inside Looking Out

We can also learn to be advocates for different attitudes. Now, no one likes a know-it-all or a contrarian, and one of the worst things we can do as we try to get better is point out how sick everyone else is. But there are subtler ways we can effect change. If we're at a party and a group of men start talking about work, we can steer the conversation toward travel or family or almost anything else. Now this can be harder than it sounds, because as you probably know, you can talk about almost anything and there are certain people who will inevitably steer it toward work. As I said, even though we can change ourselves, we probably aren't going to change the world. But even small victories make our own healing process better. And for those who are borderline workaholics, those little reminders that there is more to life than talking about work can make all the difference in the world.

Going Deeper

For many of us, focusing on day-to-day routines and moment-to-moment decisions will not be enough. We cannot answer all the questions that plague us while we're at our desks, or wherever our workplaces may be. Introspection on an intercontinental flight doesn't really work, especially when our laptop computers are open and staring at us. But we can take a short look at our life while we're at our desks. When faced with one of those moments when the virtue of work is thrust in our face, or when we're trapped in a work-related conversation we don't want to be in at a social event, we can get away for a little bit. We can touch base with our values for just a moment and remind ourselves what really matters:

How much money is enough money?

What are my real priorities?

What are (were) my dreams?

What do I want to remember about my life during my old age?

What do I believe in? A higher power? If not, what is my place on earth?

Who do I love? How do I show it? When was the last time I told them I loved them?

Who are my friends?

Can you be one thing at work—a dedicated, hard-driving guy who accomplishes more than the rest—and, in turn, can you then turn off that need to strive, to achieve, to be on top, at home? How can you strike that balance?

This is all about setting boundaries for yourself. It's about being conscious. When is the meter running and when are you off duty? Self-assessment is at the root of our problem with work. Running on autopilot is our greatest enemy. What we need to really do, in order to find out what we want, is be prepared to ask ourselves at any given moment: WHAT DO I WANT? WHAT DO I WANT TO BE? WHAT IS IMPORTANT, REALLY IMPORTANT TO ME? This self-survey isn't earth shattering. And you probably will come up with your own questions that keep you going. It might not be much, but it will help you rebuild your relationships, regain some key perspective on your work, and begin to pull yourself out of the terrible rut you've been creating. And most of all, it's a start. If we don't take the time to attempt to define ourselves, then others will do it for us.

Ideally, you'll learn more about why you feel you need to be a Player at work, and you'll figure out that you can do your job well without the adrenaline rush that comes with seeing yourself first and foremost as that Player. As you move toward change, your first goal should at least be to stop being a Player at home. To want to be "listened to," cared for, made to laugh, to be held, to be loved more than to be important. If all you know is your work, you have nothing to offer those at home.

We all know how hard it is to switch gears from the chaos we know at work to the chaos at home. If you're work-weary when you reach the door, you won't have an ounce of patience, or the inclination to sit down and listen. If you need time to yourself before you transfer to "home life," then take it. Go off by yourself. Ponder the day. Think about what's truly important. Don't bring the pressure cooker home with you. Give yourself permission to download.

Now let's pay attention to balancing life outside the office.

Chapter 7

Now That I'm Here, Where Am I?:

Finding and Preserving Your Relationship

with Yourself, Your Partner,

Family, and Friends

The great secret of success is to go through life as a man who never gets used up.

—Albert Schweitzer

What matters is how you choose to love. As you know, there's a lot of emphasis placed on success, and I hear it all the time. But what I know is there is no success where there is no joy, so instead of looking for success in your life, look for the thing that is going to bring you the greatest joy. Joy is the only goal really worth seeking.

—Oprah Winfrey

Creating a balance in your day doesn't just mean you hide your calendar, turn off your cell phone, unplug the fax machine, and turn all your clocks to the wall. Obviously, to make these changes, you have to go deep. It takes time, and those with whom you are close can help you make the transitions in your day-to-day life.

Putting People First

When you first realized that you'd dug yourself into a well, you may have felt very alone. But the path to recovery shouldn't be a lonely one. Now is the time to rebuild all those connections with the people you care about the most, to remind yourself of what you're working for. This is one of the hardest things to do, because it means you have to face your own failures with the ones you love; you've hurt or neglected the people who've meant the most to you. You may encounter resistance at first, but you can rebuild those bridges you thought you burned.

Before you set out to reconnect with others, remember what pilots tell airline passengers about using oxygen masks. Before you attempt to assist anyone around you, you need to put the oxygen mask on yourself first.

Reconnecting with Yourself

The workaholic, like other addicts, never really takes the time for any self-examination or introspection. One of the reasons we immerse ourselves in work, as I've discussed earlier, is our need to evaporate; to turn the mirrors to the wall. Can you remember what your true passions were before you got trapped—or trapped yourself? Was it baseball? Reading? Gardening? Skiing? Whatever it was, try to revisit it. I've just recently gone back to my old record collection—and I have a big one. I'm choosing which of these old 45s to take to a place where they rerecord them and burn them into a CD (or CDs, in my case). It's been fun, and I've even begun reading about the history of many of the singers and musicians who made those wonderful recordings.

Think about the positive themes in your life: the music you love, the humor you find your own. Reflect on days past when you felt a greater sense of wonderment. You may have to do some time tracking back to childhood. So what? Take aimless walks. They all end up somewhere.

One of the most important parts of becoming a whole person again is finding out who that person is. When we realize how sick we are, the person we've become can seem pretty small, pretty sad. We've built ourselves up with our work, but when we find out our work is destroying us, we lose that part of our identity. I remember that when I first confronted my disease, I was faced with how empty my car and my house made me feel. Or rather, that without those important bits of status propping up my ego and identity, I didn't have much of an identity left.

That was one of the scariest moments in my life. But from there on, it got better. Because when I started looking back on the other parts of my life, I saw that while I had risked losing a lot, I still had much to be grateful for: friends, family, two extraordinary children. I was amazed any of them still wanted anything to do with me. But once I shed some of the self-pity of those early weeks, I saw a lot of promise, and no shortage of good things I had done. My life wasn't a waste, nor was I.

Take a look back—what were your weakest, darkest times? Did you begin to take on additional addictive behaviors? If you did, do they continue now? Try to tackle them one at a time. You may need to seek out a professional therapist for help. You'll begin to distinguish when you're in your workaholic mode and when you're not. This new self-awareness will begin to set you free.

It's time to think more about how you feel about yourself. In Appendix A, you'll find the Twelve Steps of Workaholics Anonymous. Look at them daily. You will need to remind yourself of your priorities and boundaries. An entire range of new thought patterns, behaviors, and possibilities will begin to emerge. You'll begin to feel positive about what's ahead for you. Your optimism will return as you begin to accept support from loved ones and professionals alike.

And here's a bonus that all of us workaholics can never hear too often: your work will be of a higher quality; you'll gradually become more productive and more valuable to your employer. This is the wonderful paradox of getting well. Your self-image will begin to improve. You'll become healthier and find yourself seeking out activities that will improve your stamina, focus, and openness. You'll begin to shed old rut-driven routines. Happiness and a sense of completeness will begin to snowball.

Other life changes will come into view. You may want to explore your own spirituality. If you agree that there is a higher power, be it your idea of God, Allah, the Sun, whomever or whatever, it will help enable you to come to grips with your disease. You will know that without help you are powerless against your addiction to work, so you must look toward a whole host of support systems, and your brand of spirituality will be one pillar.

Coupled with this newfound openness comes a sense of humility. You've experienced that "power high" when you're immersed in work. Power is largely mythical, at least in most workplaces. If you are power-hungry and driven to control, now is the time to pull back and realize that the power you felt was really a certain kind of tyranny for yourself and those around you. Now is the time to find substitutes for that need for power, positive things you can do in your life that give you the same kind of satisfaction. It won't be easy and it won't happen right away. But without building yourself up again, you will be vulnerable to relapsing into your own power-hungry ways.

I've become more physically active, and the better I feel and look, the better I feel about myself. But don't get caught up in turning exercise into another form of competition with yourself or others. I'm talking about actually enjoying the freedom and good health that physical activity brings—the results of becoming "whole."

Reconnecting with Your Partner

If you've hidden behind your work for any length of time, you've abandoned your partner. While she (or he) may have learned to cope with your invisibility, your partner is usually lonely, bereft, and without any identity in terms of being part of a "couple."

The first thing you need to do is acknowledge that you haven't been available, that you've been an invisible man. This is very hard to do. You'll be tempted to leap in to justify your behavior, to sugar-coat it. It's very hard to say, "I haven't been there for you, and I'm sorry." "I let my job be more important to me than you, and I'm sorry." "You needed and deserved an equal partner, and I've been making you do all the heavy lifting. I'm sorry."

None of this is going to come as any earth-shattering news to your partner. You've probably been talking about this for a while, or at least hearing from her that you haven't been around for her. What's new is that you're acknowledging it, apologizing for your past behavior, and next asking for help. "I want to be a better partner for you, but I've dug myself into a hole and I need your help getting out of it." Men are famous for not wanting to ask for help. We've all heard the jokes about us never stopping to ask directions when we're lost on the highway. I don't know why, but it's hard for us to admit that we can't do it all by ourselves. But we have to ask for help, both because we need it and because our partners want to know that we really do need them too.

Will you find resistance? Probably. Your partner won't know how to react—she's been soloing for so long. Remember, she has blamed your "career" and your job and your work for your disappearance and lack of interest. Rabbi and marriage counselor M. Gary Neuman, author of *Helping Your Kids Cope with Divorce the Sandcastles Way*, talks about our tendency to create more of our intimacy within our work environment. Do you circulate the funny e-mails you get to your coworkers but not to your wife? Do you hang out at the coffee machine to chat up your colleagues but clam up when you get home to your wife because you just need a few moments of peace and quiet? If you've been saving more of your emotional investment for your coworkers than for your partner, she has every right to feel like you've been screwing around on her, only with your job instead of another woman. She's been deeply hurt, and it's going to take time to heal that.

I was really lucky to have Wendy as a partner. My wife, and still my business partner, has her feet planted on the floor and doesn't fight gravity. Where I tend to be the dreamer, she tends to be the more practical one—and her grounded guidance helped get us through a very rough period. It was very hard for me to open up to her, and very hard to hear back how abandoned and alone she'd felt, but we were able to start talking and keep talking. She knew how hard it was for me to admit I needed her help, and she didn't slam the door on me, although I wouldn't have blamed her if she had.

You have to realize that you may not get through this necessary transition alone. In my case, my wife was my ultimate savior. She and I kept talking until we felt we were back on the road to healthy work and home life. You may need couples therapy or marriage counseling if you can't talk it out together. A qualified counselor can help the two of you acknowledge each other's feelings and create a safe environment to air all the caustic emotions that have been building. A good counselor can talk to the two of you separately and in joint sessions and help you build bridges until you're on solid enough footing to work the rest of it out together. Ironically, it can be easier to open up to a stranger than to your own partner; a counselor is an unbiased, nonjudgmental third party whose neutrality can help you see your own prejudices and assumptions. I know a lot of couples whose partnerships have been saved by counseling. Don't be afraid to seek it out if you need it.

The two things your partner has been missing are your time and your attention. The first thing I'd encourage you to do is make the time to do things together. Your goal is both to get away from your place of work, obviously, but also to get away from home. It is, after all, one of the places you fled, at some point.

Think back to when you were in your courting days with your partner. You didn't take her for granted then. You plotted and planned to take her to the right movie or show, mapped out a romantic walk, got together the right bunch of friends. Now's the time to put yourself back in that dating mode. See movies, take long drives, go to the seashore, or visit the neighbors, family members, old friends. If you've got kids, remember that hiring the babysitter is work too—why don't *you* pick up the phone and make the arrangement? (If you don't even know where the list of sitters is, make it your business to find out, and commit to hiring a babysitter yourself as often as you can. You might want to try to make a standing arrangement with a sitter every two weeks or so.) Take responsibility for planning time together away from the pressures of work and home. If you can't get away from the house, turn off the phone and computer. Have an evening when no interruptions are allowed. You don't have to spend a pack of money to have a great evening; a video from the library and a home-cooked meal (how about you make it?) are a great break.

It may sound so easy, so pat, but in short, these are simple ways to begin to become engaged in life with your partner again.

Or maybe this all sounds so corny and self-conscious, or forced and unromantic. If so, remember, you've already learned that if you don't plan for these times, they just don't happen. Stop putting such a premium on spontaneity. Your partner won't become a high priority for you unless you plan to make that happen.

And when you're with your partner, really be there. Attention must be paid. If you catch yourself worrying about work in the middle of a date with your wife or your partner don't beat yourself up, but just push those thoughts aside and refocus on what's important. The truth is, you won't always have the luxury of making all the time you want to be with your partner; the realities of work are going to intrude from time to time. Your goal is to take the time you do have with your partner and really be available emotionally as well as physically.

Just as you'll backslide, remember that your partner also has established patterns of behavior. And while your partner wants you to get better, remember that it's ultimately your fight you're fighting. We have to be mindful not to get impatient with our wives (or families or friends) when they wonder what happened to the old go-getter you. It's hard to change around people, and sometimes the people you are closest to have the hardest time with the shift. Your partner may well have invested a lot of time in a different world of friends and support—and you may not fit into that world. Your goal is to integrate yourself more fully with your partner while respecting her other interests and friendships.

It is, of course, in the best interest of those close to you to be accepting of your new choices, and, ultimately they will welcome them. Remember, though, that your partner has suffered through a lot of tough times without you, literally and figuratively. They've been cleaning up after you, making excuses on your behalf, and generally living an emotionally barren life. Give them time to adjust; you, too will need time to change.

Reconnecting with Your Kids

One of the biggest changes I've made is to get to know my kids as people, not just as things I was supposed to provide for. This took a lot of doing, since, as I've described, Michael and Ross had long since learned to count me out as an available parent. They went to Mom for just about everything, in part because they knew she'd be there for them, and in part because I'd made it so clear that I was an

Important Guy with Important Work that they were some-times afraid to interrupt me to ask for some of my time. I couldn't tell you who their teachers were, sometimes not even what grade they were in. I'm sure I couldn't name all of their friends. I let Wendy do all the birthday and Christmas shopping for them, plan all the parties, and make all the playdates. When I finally decided to take a close accounting of how much I really knew about not just the humdrum, routine details of their lives, but what their hopes and dreams were, I was ashamed at how much I'd missed out on.

Little by little, we've rebuilt those connections. One of the best ways to reintegrate yourself into your kids' lives is to get involved in their activities and interests. Ross is a budding meteoroloist; Michael is a rock music lover and creator of video games. Ross and Mike have a great time playing video games together, and I like to take them on, although I don't think I'll ever beat either one of them. Ross is also an oboeist who plays in the Greater Twin Cities Youth Symphony. I go to all his concerts and try to catch as many rehearsals as I can. I feel unbelievably proud of what he's accomplished. And the big difference between now and those school concerts all those years ago is that I don't find myself yearning to bolt away, checking my watch and tapping my toes with impatience. And I certainly don't make myself and Wendy go in separate cars to get home ten minutes earlier!

Michael and I love to play cards and Balderdash, talk politics, and see movies. He's smart and his own person, an iconoclast who loves adventure, challenge, and ideas. His path through life will be completely different from mine— it won't be in any way linear. It will be fascinating to see where time and his talent take him.

One of my greatest challenges has been learning to listen, really listen, to my kids. I realized that I'd unconsciously imported my expectations from the workplace to home, and I approached childrearing with standards that made a lot of sense at the office but none at all at home. I had to learn that a lot of times when my kids talked with me, they weren't looking for me to charge in and solve their problems; they just wanted a sympathetic ear and some acknowledgment. I had to learn to find my kids' own rhythms and work within those instead of imposing my own. They're teaching me daily about the value of patience. If you need some guidance in this area too, I've recommended some helpful parenting books in Appendix B.

One of the most poignant revelations my sons have made to me is that the whole time I was beavering away to make the big bucks to buy them more things, they really didn't even want them. As it turned out, my sons were often embarrassed by any sign of affluence. I'd actually bought Michael a BMW for his sixteenth birthday (although at least I had the insight to be remorseful about it afterward and didn't buy Ross a car). I later found that they didn't want me to drive them anywhere in my latest-model Mercedes Benz; they'd beg me to drop them off at the back door or the end of the driveway at a friend's house so the friend wouldn't see how show-offy their dad was. I'd slaved to buy this beautiful home, and it turned out that the boys were sometimes reluctant to bring friends there for playdates; they felt self-conscious about such an obvious display of wealth. What could be more ironic?

Ross finally said it in so many words: "You don't have to repeat what your father did. We don't want you to do that." My family has been so forgiving of how deeply I fell into the very same Invisible Man pit my dad had fallen into, and it's because of their love that I've finally dug my way out of it.

As the father of two sons, I don't feel I can speak adequately to the differing needs of the father/daughter relationship. So I was delighted to come across an organization called Dads and Daughters (DADs), whose executive director is Joe Kelly, the man who created and edited *New Moon*, the magazine for and by young girls. DADs' credo is "Being true to our daughters so they can be true to themselves." (For more information, check out *www.dadsanddaughters.org.*) DADs has a wonderful questionnaire to help fathers quantify the extent of their involvement in their daughter's lives. If you're the father of a daughter, take the following quiz:

How Am I Doing as My Daughter's Father?

To get a sense of where your relationship with your daughter could use improvement, answer the following questions as honestly as you can with "often," "sometimes," or "hardly ever."

	Often	Some-times	Hardly Ever
1. I can name her three best friends.	1	2	3
2. I take my daughter to school.	1	2	3
3. I volunteer to help her with her extracurricular activities.	1	2	3
4. I know my daughter's goals.	1	2	3
5. I comment on my wife/ partner's weight.	3	2	1
6. I'm physically active with my daughter (shoot hoops, jog, etc.).	1	2	3
7. I make dinner for my family.	1	2	3
8. I visit my daughter's school during the school day.	1	2	3
9. I take my daughter to work with me.	1	2	3

	Often	Some-times	Hardly Ever
10. I talk to my daughter about managing money.	1	2	3
11. I spend a half hour one-on-one with my daughter doing something we both enjoy.	1	2	3
12. I talk to other fathers about raising kids.	1	2	3
13. I talk to other fathers about raising daughters.	1	2	3
14. I restrict her activities in order to protect her.	3	2	1
15. I talk to my daughter about advertising.	1	2	3
16. I tell my daughter what her strengths are.	1	2	3
17. I comment on my daughter's weight.	3	2	1
18. I know what school project she's working on.	1	2	3
19. I protest negative media portrayals of girls.	1	2	3
20. I view pornographic material.	3	2	1

	Often	Some-times	Hardly Ever
21. I participate in parenting organizations.	1	2	3
22. I yell at my daughter's mother.	3	2	1
23. I suggest my daughter go on a diet.	3	2	1
24. I object when others suggest that she go on a diet.	1	2	3
25. I converse with my daughter, and she does most of the talking.	1	2	3
26. I know what my daughter is concerned about today.	1	2	3
27. I know how many student government officers at her school are girls.	1	2	3
28. I have read her school's sexual harassment policy.	1	2	3
29. I help boys learn to respect girls.	1	2	3
30. I tell my daughter stories about my own youth.	1	2	3

Total Points:

If you scored

30–35: Your relationship with your daughter looks like it's on very solid ground.

36–45: You appear to have a good foundation, but there are places to improve.

46–60: You probably need active steps to reexamine your attitudes and learn ways to build deeper respect for each other.

61–90: It's time to consider a serious change. Your actions and attitudes may be undermining your daughter.

How Does My Daughter Think I'm Doing as Her Father?

Now give the quiz to your daughter and ask her to fill it out, based on what she has observed about you. Then exchange answers and discuss the results. You may be amazed at what comes up.

Protecting Our Kids from Workaholism

In getting to know our sons and daughters, we can reclaim the chance to be good role models for them and instill in them the values that will help protect them from falling into the traps we know so well. We can start by teaching our children that there is more than getting good grades or being captain of a team or first chair in the school orchestra. The expectations we place on children can be tremendous, and I fear we are raising a whole new generation of workaholics.

We all talk about how much homework our children have. School districts have heated discussions about whether more homework equates with more achievement. Tell someone your kid has twenty minutes a night, and they'll tell you their kid has at least an hour. Or two. Bragging about how hard your kid works has become a kind of sick competitive sport.

"Minimum of three hours a night, Sometimes five or six. I guess that's what will get him into the right college, though."

This is always said in a semiboastful way, as if our children were mirror images of us, and virtuous in the extreme for working on into the night. Every night.

It's so easy to fall into this trap. Tell yourself that you don't care how well your kid does in school, that you only care if your child is happy—then take your emotional temperature when another parent tells you their kid got straight A's, or got into the gifted program, or aced the SATs, or got into Harvard. Were you honestly happy for them, or did you feel some twinges? Check that reaction, and watch yourself to see if you're transmitting the kinds of values you really want your child to have. If you're telling your child to value kindness and community and loving relationships above all else, but you're hiring tutors, restricting privileges for less-than-stellar grades, and centering most conversations around achievement, then you're sending a mixed message that points your child toward workaholism.

We have to show our kids that we live our own values if we want them to emulate those values. Honoring your family first, and showing it in word and deed, sends that powerful message.

My relationship with Wendy gets better almost daily; she's truly a loving life partner with whom I can share anything. I feel like I'm living less on the outside and much more on the inside. I feel more a part of the family, more a part of the daily routine. I'm very much more aware of what everyone's doing, who has a football game, who has a baseball game. Better yet, I'm finding real life in those very details. It's the day-to-day things that are most important.

Reconnecting with Your Friends

This has been a real test for me—reconnecting with old friends, and trying to make new ones. The first inclination when men get together after a long absence is to talk about work. Right off the bat: "So, how's the job? Did you get that promotion? Is your boss still there, and is he still a jerk?" and on and on. It seems to be the most favored way to start any kind of conversation.

A couple of weeks ago, I saw a friend with whom I was

very close some time ago. We didn't talk about his medical practice. We didn't talk about my literary and talent agency. We talked about his daughters, and I talked about my sons. We talked about music. We talked about movies. And I was conscious of skirting the work issues and the absence of them in our conversation every minute. But I really enjoyed our time together. I felt relieved at not having to talk about my work—talking about it resubmerges you in it—and it felt good "catching up" with him about the things that were most important to both of us.

I did something else that's helped me a lot: I joined a men's group. I was first invited to join this group through someone with whom I worked about ten years ago. I declined. At the time I thought, *What a waste of time. These guys are all sitting around bitching about their work or their wives.* I didn't know which was less appealing, but I knew it wasn't for me. Well, I was wrong as I could be.

Some of these "men's groups" are born out of AA (Alcoholics Anonymous) meetings, or group therapy, or just a number of guys who know one another from church or family connections. Mine is composed of about ten men roughly my age, at the same socioeconomic level, all of whom are married. We have great commonalities of experience, and there's a genuine fraternal feeling among us. We are more alike than unalike—which is true of just about everyone on earth—but a concept foreign to workaholics who see themselves as "different" and as "lone wolves."

I really look forward to getting together with these guys. Yes, we're kind of a "support" group, but we're also just plain friends. There's a lot of laughter, a lot a great story-telling, some talk about work (but we keep that to a minimum, unless one of us is seeking solace or advice about a problem), and now we're planning trips that we can take together as a group, as well as some with our wives and partners. Here's the best part: we're all "successful," but we have vastly different personal "stories"—our life experiences have somehow drawn us together, but I revel in hearing how each of the men in the group got to the same place I did.

Not everyone is a "group" kind of guy. That's fine. You can reinvestigate old friendships on a one-on-one basis, too. And before you use that line we've all used about ten million times: "Let's get together some time after work or on the weekend"—but we never do—let yourself realize that, yes, indeed, you can. It doesn't take a miracle, and it doesn't have to take up an entire evening or weekend. It sure helps to get yourself "out of your own head" by getting into someone else's. It's enriching, it's fun, it's interesting, and it creates a more humane, multidimensional person—you.

Reconnecting with Your Community

One surefire way of getting your mind away from yourself and work is to volunteer in a church, temple, hospital, school, shelter, or any other institution that needs hands, arms, and hearts. Get rid of the idea that one person's efforts can't make a difference and that such pursuits are a waste of time. They are time better spent than at work.

A while ago, I started volunteering at a local hospital. I bring magazines and books around to patients and people in the waiting room; I check in with the patients to see if they need anything. None of this qualifies for the Albert Schweitzer humanitarian award, but it makes me feel wonderful. I feel like I'm doing something small but genuinely helpful, and it makes me feel good about myself and more connected to my community. I also volunteer my time to speak at publishing and writer's conferences. It's intellectually stimulating and reminds me why I got into this business in the first place.

Get your friends and family to volunteer with you. It's a different kind of high—a healthy high. It's all about connection.

Numerous scientific studies have demonstrated the protective effect that being an active part of the community confers. Men who stay connected to family, friends, and community have fewer heart attacks and report a higher quality of life. Sure, the health benefit is nice, but do this because it'll bring you more joy than you could imagine.

Freedom and Tyranny

I promise you, you will be tempted to slip and go back to your old ways. Some will actually expect it of you, thinking, "You got over the flu, now let's get back to work." Expect this, and plan for it.

I believe (and I have strong evidence to support this) that the quality of my work has become far better—I rarely slip back into frantic behavior: putting fires out all day, being totally defensive about not having completed a task. So I look at that, and it feels good, and I'm not as stressed, or as angry, or as depressed. I also have noticed that things are easier—I don't feel like Sisyphus, pushing the rock up the mountain every day. And I'm getting encouragement from my family, friends, and coworkers. That's a great, freeing feeling. Focus on your steps forward, not your lapses. Remember to stay positive.

When I was deep in my workaholism, I would keep exhaustive to-do lists. These lists were ridiculous, filled with everything I needed to do for the month. Looking at them, I would panic. So much to do (more than anyone could do in a year, in some cases) and no time to do it in! Now I still use to-do lists, but I keep them very simple. And I make sure that each to-do list only has enough for the day. I also try to make sure that the things on the top of the list aren't even work related. I might remind myself to call my wife during the day for a chat, or take my kids out for a movie in the middle of the week. But most important of all, I focus on the day at hand and try not to let work govern the natural rhythm of my day.

Inevitably, you will get "called back" to old patterns of behavior. There will always be a "special project" or a need to cover for an absent coworker. React to these situations not with obsessive dedication, but rather with flexibility.

Don't fall for the tyranny of freedom. When we feel "free," burdenless, or with time on our hands, those of us who are recovering must not let this time tyrannize us. Enjoy the downtime; don't try to fill it up. These are contradictory concepts, and they should be seen as such. Remember your newfound priorities, and begin to enjoy the freedom you've found within them. As author Dr. Anne Wilson Schaef wisely says, "Life is living in process. Life is fluid. Life is change."

At the risk of sounding gloomy or priggish, I have to warn you about the temptations of other forms of escape. It's easy, as we're climbing out of the trough of workaholism, to get what seems like a leg up from drugs or alcohol or sex. But we have to be mindful that there are dangers in any of these pursuits as well. Do we have to become Jesuits to live healthfully? Of course not. But if you find yourself having a couple of drinks every night to ease some of the anxiety of those extra hours at home, then you're not quite as healed as you think.

It's a long, long road. Remind yourself of that and it

makes it a little easier. Just like that first realization that you're sick is the first step to getting better, understanding the long and hard road ahead is a component to coping with how difficult recovery is.

I've made a lot of progress, but I'm certainly not immune to rolling back to my old behaviors. Sometimes I catch myself sneaking away from a family gathering "just to check my e-mail." Who am I kidding? I'm not waiting for a kidney donor or a note from Publishers Clearinghouse telling me they're on the way over. I have an American Express Platinum card, so Amex sends me its glossy *Departures* magazine, which advertises extraordinary—and extraordinarily expensive—vacations. I'll catch myself telling my wife, "Gee, I can afford this if I pick up that piece of business." Of course, the spectre of paying for my kids' college tuition can get me in a lather in a nanosecond. I try not to be so materialistic, then I see the latest-model Mercedes-Benz and I "have to have it." It takes a lot of willpower to say no to those "have to haves," and I still screw up.

Laugh at yourself when you start slipping—even a little bit—but be mindful that "one drink leads to emptying the bottle."

Integration

Combining the components of our lives can be difficult. We've gotten so used to multitasking that it's hard to slow down and give our full attention to one thing at a time. In order to create some semblance of balance in our lives, we need to be good at shifting gears.

Integrating our days with play, recreation, and social interaction, whatever we want to do that is decidedly not work, will lead to a longer life, a better, more fulfilling marriage or intimate relationship, solid friendships, new and rewarding relationships with our children, and, more than likely, far fewer internal struggles. When we let go of the myth that work equals nobility, we will have time to fully live our lives, without fear of failure, regret, anger, and resentment.

One of your greatest successes will come on the day when you look back at your time on the job and shrug. "How was your day at work?" someone might ask you, and your answer, without having to think about it, will be: "It was a day." No need to dramatize the daily battles or crow about the successes. This attitude doesn't mean you're slacking off or not doing your job anymore. It simply means you aren't carrying your job around with you all the time.

And you don't need to dread work either. For a lot of us, what got us into trouble in the first place was that work was fun. It gave us a rush. We can find that rush again, as long as we don't depend on it. I find that I still love making deals and signing clients and helping authors get published. Just because I'm a recovering workaholic doesn't mean I have to be afraid of doing my job. But every time I make that deal,

I also remind myself that there is so much more to life, that I don't live to make deals, but that making deals is how I pay for everything else that is so important to me.

Gone Fishing

I used to actually lie to people when I was about to take a vacation. I was so certain that time off was frivolous and indicated weakness that I wouldn't admit that I either wanted or needed time off. I was also worried that I'd be "found out," very much worried about "missing" something; what if I wasn't at work and something important happened? I wasted so much time and energy in not being productive but working endless hours, instead of taking a break and recharging my batteries. I know better now.

Even while on "vacation," I'd call the office (sometimes secretly) several times a day. Expecting a work-related catastrophe, I couldn't pull myself away. Little by little and over several years, I've begun to take real time off. That means, in some cases, going to remote resorts with no phones, televisions, or radios. It's worked wonders. I take books and my family. Period. I've been looking more and more forward to those trips over the past decade. I've learned to sleep better. I've gotten to know my children even better.

A couple of years back, during our kids' spring break,

we went to Hawaii, to Kauai and the Big Island. We fell in love (who wouldn't?). It's heaven only four hours west of L.A. We thoroughly enjoyed our eight days. But on the eve of our flight back to the mainland—back to school for the boys, and back to work for us parents—we looked at one another and said, "We need another week." And we took it. I felt not a glimmer of tension, but relief. I knew the office would still be there, the problems, as well as the triumphs; the house was being tended to. And I needed that time, and I didn't for one second feel that I shouldn't have taken it. I don't think my wife, kids, and I will ever forget that precious extra week we took for ourselves. When we got home, we were happy, well rested, and at our best. You need to claim some time off for yourself and recognize it as a necessity, as essential to your health and well-being as air and food. You don't need to fly all the way to Hawaii; you can find a retreat at a friend's cabin up north, a rustic inn out in the country, or even in your own backyard. The idea is to affirm why you're working by taking a break from work.

I have come to believe that the more leisure time we take, the more effective we are at our jobs. We're more satisfied, more creative, and energetic. The irony of the man who mistakes his job for a life is that he creates no life even in his job.

My cousin Tim plays for work. Let me explain: he is now an administrator at the National Outdoor Leadership School in Wyoming. Tim is smart; he loved the outdoors, was a strong sportsman, enjoyed animals and nature, so he "went fishing" for a job. I won't suggest that he doesn't work—in the traditional sense—but he has found a way to blend his passions with a career. It wasn't just "Do what you love and the money will follow." He doesn't do it for the money. He does it because he loves it, and he knows when to quit. But the blend is a perfect example of how some of us can find that balance in both our world of work and our life that surrounds it.

I'm getting back to my love of art, long dormant. I had traded my oils and brushes for a laptop and a phone. Now I'm back to painting, and I feel I have some new balance.

The point of all this self-disclosure is to illustrate that you, too, can break the chain of workaholism. It doesn't happen overnight, and it's not like quitting alcohol. It's not all or nothing, either. Once a workaholic, you have those tendencies for life. As you create things to look forward to (no, not another marketing meeting), such as travel, creating a collection of things you enjoy, or reading for pleasure, make a habit of asking yourself every single morning: "What would I really like to do today?" This is not about fantasy. We're not talking about jumping into bed with Nicole Kidman. I'm talking about making certain that you enjoy a portion of your day, every day. I'm saying, apportion your workload and don't let what's on your plate at the office overwhelm you. Don't get lost again behind the desk, or wherever you work. By now I hope you know it's just not worth it. As the saying goes, "When I'm on my deathbed, I don't think my last regret will be, 'I wish I had spent more time at work.' "

I have given myself a gift, but I had plenty of help. I've gotten to know my children and my wife, my friends—some new, some old. And every day, I try to say goodbye to who I was and why I was that way.

Enjoy your journey home.

Sitting in the Midday Sun

I'm sitting by the side of the river
Underneath the pale blue sky
I've got no need to worry, I'm in no hurry
I'm lookin' at the world go by.

Just sitting in the midday sun
Just soakin' up that currant bun
With no particular purpose or reason
I'm sittin' in the midday sun.

Everybody says I'm lazy
They all tell me get a job, you slob
But I'd rather be a poor boy, walkin' round with
*   nothin'*
Than a rich man scared of losing all he's got.

So I'm just sitting in the midday sun
Just soakin' up that currant bun
Why should I have to give my reasons
For sitting in the midday sun.

Ooh, look at all the ladies
Lookin' their best in their summer dresses
Sittin' in the sun, I got no place to go, I got no one
But who needs a job when it's sunny.

I haven't got a steady occupation
I can't afford a telephone
And I haven't got a stereo, radio or video
Mortgage, overdraft or bank loan.

The only way that I can get my fun
Is by sitting in the midday sun
With no particular purpose or reason
I'm sitting in the midday sun.

Oh, listen to the people
Who say I'm a failure and I've got nothin'
Oh if they would only see, I've my pride, I've got no
*   money*
But who needs a job when it's sunny.

Everybody thinks I'm crazy
And everybody says I'm dumb

But when I see the people shoutin' at each other
I'd rather be an out-of-work bum.

So I'm just sitting in the midday sun
Just soakin' up that currant bun
With no particular purpose or reason
I'm sitting in the midday sun.

—RAY DAVIES, *PRESERVATION, ACT ONE*

Appendix A

The Twelve Steps of

Workaholics Anonymous

Maybe your kneejerk reaction when you read the words "twelve steps" is to say that this has nothing to do with you. You associate any kind of twelve-step program with Alcoholics Anonymous or some kind of New Age nonsense.

Before you dismiss it so quickly, do a little more soul searching. As a literary agent, I work with a lot of authors who specialize in research into addictive behavior, and they confirm that many people who are workaholics have other addictions as well: to alcohol, drugs, sex, even exercise. Take a good look at yourself. After a long day at the office, do you need a few drinks to unwind? Any recreational drugs? Do you take the same attitudes you use in the workplace and apply them to other activities? This isn't an easy thing to quantify. As I've said before, it isn't that x

many drinks makes you an alcoholic, and *y* many drinks doesn't. It's about taking a closer look at how and why you indulge in certain behaviors, and whether or not you truly have control over yourself.

Don't get hung up on labels here. This is about helping you help yourself.

Even if you don't see yourself as addicted to other behaviors, look at the twelve steps below, which have been adopted by the organization called Workaholics Anonymous. They can be very helpful in guiding you as you work to recover and achieve more balance and joy in your life. As with any twelve-step program, Workaholics Anonymous begins by challenging you to admit that you have a problem, to take full responsibility for it, and to seek help.

The Twelve Steps of Workaholics Anonymous

1. We admitted we were powerless over our compulsive working, that our lives had become unmanageable.
2. We came to believe that a power greater than ourselves would restore us to sanity.
3. We made a decision to turn our will and our lives over to the care of God as we understood Him.
4. We made a searching and fearless moral inventory of ourselves.
5. We admitted to God, to ourselves, and to another human being the exact nature of our wrongs.

6. We became entirely ready to have God remove all those defects of character.

7. We humbly asked Him to remove our shortcomings.

8. We made a list of all persons we had harmed, and became willing to make amends to them all.

9. We made direct amends to such people wherever possible, except when to do so would injure them or others.

10. We continued to take personal inventory, and when we were wrong, promptly admitted it.

11. We sought through prayer and meditation to improve our conscious contact with God as we understood Him, praying only for the knowledge of His will for us and the power to carry that out.

12. Having had a spiritual awakening as the result of these steps, we tried to carry this message to workaholics and to practice these principles in all our affairs.

If you don't believe in God, please substitute any other concept that feels genuine to you: appealing to a higher power, to the collective unconscious, to the best, highest part of yourself—whatever works.

I've also found the following directives, from *The Tools of Workaholics Anonymous*, published by Workaholics Anonymous through NYU Press, to be enormously helpful in putting the twelve steps to use. I recommend that you reread the list every day. In trying to put the guidelines to use, don't beat yourself up if you backslide. We all do. It took a long time for you to get to where you were; it'll take a while to get better. Be patient with yourself.

The Tools of Workaholics Anonymous

Listening. We set aside time each day for prayer and meditation. Before accepting any commitments, we ask our Higher Power and friends for guidance. We must remember that we cannot fight addiction by ourselves; we need to make positive connections every day.

Prioritizing. We decide which are the most important things to do first. Sometimes that may mean doing nothing. We strive to stay flexible to events, reorganizing our priorities as needed. We view interruptions and accidents as opportunities for growth. When one door closes, another door opens; we must be open and ready for new and inventive opportunities to come into our lives.

Substituting. We do not add a new activity without eliminating from our schedule one that demands equivalent time and energy. We must weigh and investigate tasks that can be eliminated or put on the back burner for something more pressing. We must be flexible.

Underscheduling. We allow more time than we think we need for a task or trip, allowing a comfortable margin to accommodate the unexpected. In life, there is always the unexpected. When we are in our disease, we are not bound by our calendars and commitments to allow for happenstance.

Playing. We schedule times for play, refusing to let ourselves work nonstop. We do not make our play into a work project. Patching the driveway and cleaning the garage should never be considered playing.

Concentrating. We try to do one thing at a time. Multiple tasking is strictly inadvisable unless it's breathing and sleeping.

Pacing. We work at a comfortable pace and rest before we get tired. To remind ourselves, we check our level of energy before proceeding to our next activity. We do not get wound up in our work, so we do not have to unwind. It is important not to get to the point of unwinding; that is a word that forms the basis for other self-defeating behaviors—the use of, among other things, alcohol and drugs. Unwinding needn't utilize synthetic means.

Relaxing. We do not yield to pressure or attempt to pressure others. We remain alert to the people and situations that trigger pressure in us. We become aware of our own actions, words, body sensations, and feelings that tell us we're responding with pressure. When we feel tension, we stop to reconnect to a Higher Power and others around us. In an addictive workplace, one's work addiction fuels the next, and the next. In today's especially overextended "I need it now" and when it "absolutely, positively must be there by the morning" world, this is a very important message.

Accepting. We accept the outcomes of endeavors, whatever the results, whatever the timing. We know that impatience, rushing, and insisting on perfect results only slow down our recovery. We are gentle with our efforts, knowing that our new way of living requires much practice. Judgment, from either within or without, hinders our progress; we know perfection happens only in nature, not at our workplace.

Asking. We admit our weaknesses and mistakes and ask our Higher Power and others for help. As work addicts, we are not given to asking for anything—help not being in our vocabulary. The more often you ask for help, the freer you'll feel.

Meetings. We attend WA meetings to learn how the fellowship works and to share our experience, strength, and hope with each other. You can't do it alone, but you must do it at home and with other work addicts. This is one buddy system that works.

Telephoning. We use the telephone to stay in contact with other members of the fellowship between meetings. We communicate with our WA friends before and after a critical task. Sometimes these phone sessions are like being talked down from a ledge; we can fall back into some of our old patterns of self-abuse when we have a particularly difficult work-related job to perform.

Balancing. We balance our work involvement with efforts to develop personal relationships, spiritual growth, creativity, and playful attitudes. A freer, uncluttered mind is a great field for new enlightened ideas; it is a place where good work can thrive.

Serving. We readily extend help to other workaholics, knowing that assistance to others adds to the quality of our own recovery. It is not enough to be the only healthy man in a leper colony; we must help others—it is our will, and we will want to become involved when we see the pain in others caused by work addiction.

Living in the now. We realize we are where our Higher Power wants us to be—in the here and now. We try to live each moment with serenity, joy, and gratitude.

Appendix B

For More Help

Excellent Resources to Help You Break the Chains of Work Addiction

Workaholics Anonymous

World Services Organization

P.O. Box 289

Menlo Park, CA 94026-0289

510-273-9253

Unofficial website: *http://people.ne.mediaone.net/wa2/*

A twelve-step program to help you accept the role of workaholism in your life and find the support you need to recover from it.

Axelrod, Steven D. *Work and the Evolving Self: Theoretical and Clinical Considerations.* Hillsdale, N.J.: Analytic Press, 1999.

A great book, perhaps aimed more for the clinician. Worthy of a good read; pay attention to the chapters "Work Inhibition and Work Compulsion" and "The Psychology of a Changing Workplace."

Elbing, Carol, and Alvar Elbing. *Militant Managers: How to Spot . . . How to Work With . . . How to Manage . . . Your Highly Aggressive Boss.* Burr Ridge, Ill.: Irwin Professional Publishing, 1994.

The alpha male who terrorizes, but does not motivate his pride. A look at how far the disease of workaholism can progress and, how to face a rabid boss.

Fassel, Diane. *Working Ourselves to Death: The High Cost of Workaholism and the Reward of Recovery.* San Francisco: Harper, 1990.

Fassel, coauthor with Dr. Anne Wilson Schaef of *The Addictive Organization* (San Francisco: Harper & Row, 1988), has written one of the most important books on workaholism.

Fox, Matthew. *The Reinvention of Work: A New Vision of Livelihood for Our Time.* San Francisco: HarperSanFrancisco, 1994.

One should read all of Matthew Fox's books. This one obviously strikes a loud chord for those of us addicted to work. Fox is a brilliant and uncommon thinker and writer.

Gleick, James. *Faster: The Acceleration of Just About Everything.* New York: Pantheon, 1999.

A beautifully written account of how everything in society is speeding up and why we resist the pressure to slow down, opting instead to continue to ratchet up the pace.

Goleman, Daniel, Ph.D. *Emotional Intelligence* (New York: Bantam, 1995) and *Working with Emotional Intelligence* (Bantam, 1998).

These international groundbreaking bestsellers truly changed the way millions of people think about maturation, the way we communicate, and human expectations. Two truly brilliant books everyone should have.

Hornstein, Harvey A. *Brutal Bosses and Their Prey: How to Identify and Overcome Abuse in the Workplace.* New York: Riverhead, 1996.

This roundtable book tells you how to work within the confines of tyranny that are so prevalent in places that foster workaholism.

Lazear, Jonathon. *Meditations for Men Who Do Too Much.* New York: Simon & Schuster, 1992.

I wrote this book from firsthand experience. Filled with quotes and affirmations, it's a daily companion guide to help you remember what you're up against and how you can slow it all down.

Levoy, Gregg. *Callings: Finding and Following an Authentic Life.* New York: Harmony Books, 1997.

The author is an eloquent, humane, and kind writer. No barbs, a gentler walk through lives not taken by most of us. It's wise and uplifting, and a fine book for any man or woman engaged in creating a better, more whole life for themselves.

Moyers, Bill D. *Healing and the Mind.* New York: Doubleday, 1993.

Moyers talks about the world of healing; a holistic look at improving our lifestyles and our future.

Robinson, Bryan E., Ph.D. *Chained to the Desk: A Guidebook for Workaholics, Their Fathers and Children and the Clinicians Who Treat Them.* New York: New York University Press, 1998.

A thorough look at how we get lulled into being over our heads in work and the tools that can teach us how to shed those schedules.

Robinson, Bryan E., Ph.D. *Overdoing It: How to Slow Down and Take Care of Yourself.* Deerfield Beach, Fla.: Health Communications, 1992.

A sound primer for men who do too much.

Schaef, Anne Wilson, and Diane Fassel. *The Addictive Organization.* San Francisco: Harper & Row, 1988.

The book that started the modern (late-twentieth-century) movement toward a sane workplace that can house, and make flourish, sane workers. A ritual model of a book for many books that followed. Schaef is one of our greatest humanists and thinkers. Try any of her books.

Schlesinger, Laura, Ph.D. *Ten Stupid Things Men Do to Mess Up Their Lives.* New York: Cliff Street Books, 1997.

In her trademark take-no-prisoners approach, Dr. Schlesinger talks about how we escape in work and what to do about it. Direct, simple, and to the point.

Schor, Juliet. *The Overworked American: The Unexpected Decline of Leisure.* New York: Basic Books, 1993.

An analysis of the creeping tendency of work to overtake our lives, with an emphasis on how the current generation of workers differs from earlier generations.

Excellent Books to Help You Explore the Role of Money in Your Life

Dominguez, Joseph R., and Vicki Robin. *Your Money or Your Life: Transforming Your Relationship with Money and Achieving Financial Independence.* New York: Penguin Books, 1999.

A landmark book that will help you ask the tough questions about why you need so much money and where it's going.

Kelley, Linda. *Two Incomes and Still Broke? It's Not How Much You Make, But How Much You Keep.* New York: Times Books, 1996.

Written primarily for two-income couples looking to see where all that money goes, Kelley's book offers a thoughtful look at how we spend unnecessarily to reward ourselves for working too hard or to assuage the guilt of spending less time with our loved ones.

Orman, Suze. *The 9 Steps to Financial Freedom: Practical & Spiritual Steps So You Can Stop Worrying.* New York: Crown Books, 1997.

This groundbreaking book helps you understand where you got your attitudes about money and how to appreciate the psychological power money plays in your life.

To Understand More About How to Be a Better Partner

Gottman, John M., Ph.D., and Nan Silver. *The Seven Principles for Making Marriage Work: A Practical Guide from the Country's Foremost Relationship Expert.* New York: Three Rivers Press, 1999.

Dr. Gottman's famous "Love Lab" uses rigorous scientific procedures to study the habits of married couples. Based on his work, this book distills the seven principles that will help you create a more harmonious relationship with your partner.

To Understand More About How to Be a Better Parent

Gordon, Thomas. *P.E.T.: Parent Effectiveness Training: The Proven Program for Raising Responsible Children*, rev. ed. New York: Three Rivers Press, 2000.

Based on the first nationwide parenting program, this thirtieth-anniversary edition teaches parents how to listen more effectively to kids and arrive at solutions to problems that respect kids' intelligence. This parenting classic deserves a place on every parent's shelf.

Mahony, Rhona. *Kidding Ourselves: Breadwinning, Babies, and Bargaining Power.* New York: Basic Books, 1995.

Mahony explores why couples intent on ditching traditional roles of men and women in parenting so often end up worn into that very groove—and how they can dig themselves out of it.

Dads and Daughters, Inc.

P.O. Box 3458

Duluth, MN 55803

Tel.: 888-824-3247

Fax: 218-722-4058

Website: *www.dadsanddaughters.org*

This national nonprofit organization of fathers and daughters is a wonderful resource for dads looking for practical information and support on connecting with their daughters.

Credits

About the Author

Jonathon Lazear, a literary agent, lives in Minneapolis, Minnesota. He is currently working on his first novel, *A Timeshare on the River Styx.*